Climbing from a Coach's Perspective

Hus Bozkurt

THE COACHING BIBLE
Climbing from a Coach's Perspective

Hus Bozkurt
Kent and Sussex Climbing
www.ksclimbing.co.uk

1st Edition
April 2019

Published in the EU by the Oxford Alpine Club
www.oxfordalpineclub.co.uk

ISBN for this volume 978-0-9935486-7-3

A catalogue record for this book is available from the British Library

PLEASE READ THIS!

Despite the seemingly safe environment of the indoor climbing wall, all forms of climbing contain an element of risk. The information given in this book is not a replacement for proper training and experience, and users should ensure that they are suitably qualified to undertake any training activities suggested in the text. The author and publisher accept no responsibility for any injury or loss caused as a result of using this book. Images and text contained within this book do not necessarily represent the views or opinions of the Oxford Alpine Club.

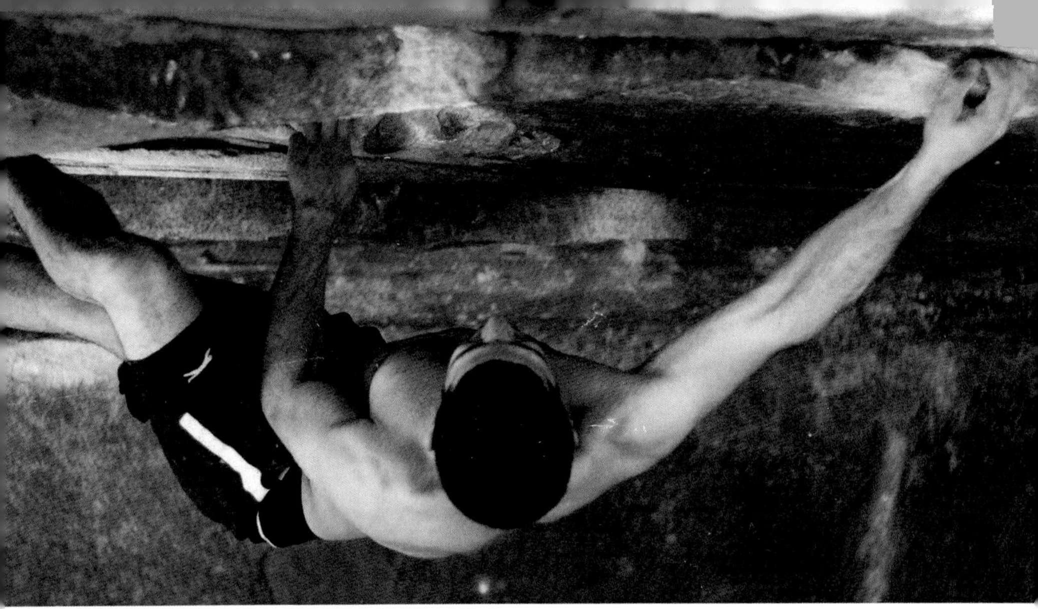

ABOUT THE AUTHOR

Hus Bozkurt is the managing director and head coach of Kent and Sussex Climbing. He began teaching outdoor climbing in 2009, and has since become a full-time climbing coach.

In 2017, Hus set up the Kent and Sussex Climbing Squad, which achieved 21 podium finishes in its first year, including a national finalist and Blokfest champion. Since then, the competition squad has gone from strength to strength and Hus now coaches climbers of a wide range of ages and abilities, including a para climbing squad, a senior squad and a masters squad.

As well as his many coaching sessions, Hus runs numerous coaching workshops with the aim of sharing ideas among the climbing coaching community. He has also developed a benchmarking system aimed specifically at the physical and training aspects of climbing.

Hus is sponsored by The Arch Climbing Wall, Beyond Hope UK, Evolv, Prana and Metolius.

ACKNOWLEDGEMENTS

I would like to thank everyone who has made this book possible. In particular: **Lizzy Simpson**, for all of the advice and help which contributed to the publication of this work, **Christopher Searle**, for helping to expand my coaching styles and development, **Mica Cutts** for help with initial design and photography, and **Ozlem Bozkurt** for initial proof-reading.

Thanks also to all of the coaches who have influenced me, including **James Jobanputra** and **Paul Widdowson**, and to **Loz Reading** for advice on team-building. I would especially like to thank everyone who I have coached, including my **competition squad**, for being great guinea pigs for an abundance of drills!

Finally, thanks to **The Arch Climbing Wall** for their support, and to **Tom Wright** for the photography.

Hus Bozkurt, May 2018

INTRODUCTION

In the long-established world of climbing, serious coaching is a relatively new discipline. Unlike most other sports, in which drills are an essential part of training, the idea of using drills to rehearse techniques in climbing is a new concept that is still finding its feet. Take professional football as an example; even at the highest standard in the sport, professional footballers do drills every single week. But why?

To answer that question, try answering these two simple problems – what is 2 + 2, and what is 124 + 92?

For the first problem you immediately know the answer is 4. You don't need to take time to visualize 2 + 2 as you already know the answer through memory. You have done the sum so many times that you don't need to think about it – it's almost habit. The second problem, on the other hand, requires you to think and work it out; it will probably take a little longer to answer.

The human brain is not actually able to multi-task, but it is really good at switching between single tasks very quickly. In climbing, if we have to focus on pinning a foot, and then have to focus on making the move to the next handhold, we are likely to stop focusing on pinning the foot as we do so. Drills, however, help conscious techniques become habits, building muscle memory which does not require mental focus. Instead, we can automatically pin the foot whenever we climb whilst focusing on something else. Since climbing is such a coordination dependant sport, each technique needs to be thoroughly practised and drilled in order to become instinctive.

Climbing is also a social and sharing-orientated sport – we love to share achievements with both friends and strangers alike. We are excited to complete a climb, but equally as excited to see our climbing partner send their project. For me, coaching is a way of sharing my love and knowledge of climbing with others. It has been the reason for my coaching career and the motivation for this book.

This book is aimed at all climbers and coaches who are looking to improve at their favourite sport. It is aimed at providing new ways of both teaching and learning techniques, with an abundance of drills to reinforce them.

THE arch
CLIMBIN
WALL
3 unique London venues.
1 membership.

WARM-UPS

When teaching climbing, it is very important to begin with a warm-up, as this will help to prevent injuries during more strenuous exercises later on.

The warm-up should always be at the very beginning of the session, and should ideally begin with pulse-raising activities to increase blood flow around the body.

The warm-up period should last for 10 to 15 minutes.

WARM-UP

Group size: 9+

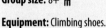

Equipment: None.

ARM BRIDGE CHALLENGE

This warm-up exercise is great fun and useful for team building too.

First, pick a volunteer and ask them to stand next to you.

Next, ask the group to stand in two lines facing each other, linking arms to create a 'bridge' along which the volunteer can pass.

Challenge the volunteer to climb along the bridge from one end of the line to the other without touching the floor.

WARM-UP

Group size: 2+

Equipment: None.

BACK TO BACK

An enjoyable warm-up exercise that also helps with team bonding.

Ask the climbers to split up into pairs and sit down back to back.

Explain to the group that on your count of three they must stand up in one motion, and then sit down again.

Repeat the exercise three or four times, then ask the pairs to carry out the same exercise again, first with their eyes shut and then without communicating with each other. Finally, ask them to complete the exercise with eyes shut, no communication, and without your count of three.

WARM-UP

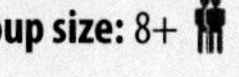

Equipment: Climbing shoes.

BOOT WARS

This lively game is a great pulse-raiser.

Find a large space and split the group into two teams, asking everyone to grab one climbing shoe.

Ask the first team to spread their shoes in a large circle, the correct way up (ie with the soles of the shoes on the floor). The second team should then place their shoes in the same circle but upside down (ie with the soles upwards).

Explain to the group that when you shout 'Go', the first team must turn all of the boots the right way up, and the second team must turn them all upside down.

WARM-UP

Group size: 4+

Equipment: None.

BUNNY HOPS RACE

An exercise that is not only great for warming up, but also really fun.

Ask the group to split up into pairs and stand behind a starting line. Designate a finishing line around eight metres from the starting line.

Explain to the group that they will race to the finish line, but can only move by bunny-hopping over each other.

Climber 1 starts by crouching on hands and knees just behind the start line. Climber 2 bunny-hops over Climber 1 by placing his or her hands on their partner's back or shoulders and leaping over them.

Climber 2 then crouches down, allowing Climber 1 to bunny-hop over them, and so on, towards the finish line. The first pair to the finish line are the winners.

WARM-UP

Group size: 2+

Equipment: None.

FINGER WARS

This entertaining game is a great pulse-raiser and is perfect for warming up the shoulders.

Find a large space and split the group into pairs.

Ask the pairs to face their partners and put their right arm forward, then link hands with their index finger pointing out.

Explain to the group that the aim of the game is to touch their opponent with their index finger.

Play two or three rounds, then swap arms.

WARM-UP

Group size: 2+

Equipment: None.

6. FOOT WARS

Similar to the previous game, this pulse-raiser is also a great exercise for a climber's legs and balance.

Find a large space and split the group into pairs. Ask each pair to stand facing each other and extend their right leg towards each other. Next, ask them to put their right foot against their opponent's right foot and explain that the objective of the game is to knock their opponent off balance without losing balance themselves.

Play two or three rounds, then swap feet.

WARM-UP

Group size: 2+

Equipment: None.

7. FROG JUMPS

Another fun warm-up exercise.

Give the climbers starting and finishing lines, approximately six metres apart.

Explain to the climbers that they will race to the finish line by 'frog jumping'. To do this, the climber should get into a full squat position with knees pointing out to the side and fingertips touching the floor in front of them.

In one motion they then leap forward without standing up, pushing with fingers and legs at the same time before landing back in the same squat position.

WARM-UP

Group size: 2+

Equipment: None.

FUN PULSE-RAISER

This easy game is a great pulse raiser, and perfect for warming up before a session.

Start by asking everyone to jog on the spot. Explain to them that you will shout out commands which they must follow.

For example, if you shout 'Jump!' they need to jump. If you shout 'Spin!' they must spin around. You can also use more imaginative commands such as:

'Dragon!' – Everyone must lie down on the floor.

'Earthquake!' – Everyone must get off the floor as quickly as possible, perhaps onto a nearby bouldering wall.

'Switch!' – Everyone must switch places with someone else.

WARM-UP

Group size: 2+

Equipment: None.

HELP UPS

This is a good warm-up for the shoulders and legs.

Split the group into pairs and have them space themselves out.

Climber 1 begins sitting down with Climber 2 standing close to them. Climber 2 grabs the hand of Climber 1 and helps them to their feet before sitting down. Climber 1 then helps Climber 2 to their feet.

Next, have both climbers sit down and hold hands, then ask them to stand up at exactly the same time.

Finally, repeat the first exercise in which Climber 2 helps Climber 1 to their feet, but this time Climber 1 should aim to make it as hard as possible for Climber 2 to do so. Repeat with Climber 1 trying to lift Climber 2 to their feet.

WARM-UP

Group size: 2+

Equipment: None.

CAUTION! – This exercise can be dangerous, and is best completed on a soft surface, clear of obstructions.

10. THE HUMAN CHAIR

A very entertaining warm-up exercise that can be quite hard work and easily used as a training exercise.

Split the group into pairs and have them space out. It is preferable for each member of the pair to be of similar build.

Explain that each pair is a team that needs to work together. Climber 1 is going to get onto Climber 2 in a hugging position, rather like a piggy back from the front, with their arms around their partner's neck, and their legs wrapped around their waist.

From this starting position, Climber 1 needs to climb over the shoulders of Climber 2, down their back and up through their legs to return to the starting position. Once they have done this they should swap roles and repeat the exercise.

WARM-UP

Group size: 4+

Equipment: None.

11. HUMAN DRAG RACE

An amusing exercise that provides a good warm-up for the legs.

Ask the group to split up into pairs and stand behind a starting line. Define a finishing line approximately seven metres from the start line.

Climber 1 starts by crossing their arms over their chest so that their hands are on their shoulders. Climber 2 then wraps their arms around Climber 1 so that their hands are by their partner's elbows.

Climber 1 leans back so that their toes are off the floor but their heels are still on the floor.

Explain to the group that they must race to the finish line, with Climber 2 dragging Climber 1 as fast as possible.

After the race, swap roles and repeat.

WARM-UP

Group size: 4+

Equipment: Slings and some other small objects such as rock shoes or tennis balls.

HUMAN PLANK CHALLENGE

This is a great exercise for building up a sweat, and is also good for team building and problem solving.

Ask the group to split into pairs and stand behind a line. Give each pair a sling and a small item such as a rock shoe or tennis ball.

The objective of the exercise is to place the object as far beyond the line as possible, without throwing or rolling it.

Explain that Climber 1 is allowed to touch the floor beyond the line only with their hands – no other part of their body can touch the floor beyond the line. Climber 2 cannot touch the floor beyond the line at all, but should assist their partner in placing the object as far past the line as they can.

WARM-UP

Group size: 6+

Equipment: None.

HUMAN PYRAMID

This drill is good fun, great for team building, and a good finish to a warm-up period.

Explain to the group that they have one minute to form a human pyramid. With larger groups this could be set as a challenge, with two groups each making pyramids side by side.

WARM-UP

Group size: 4+

Equipment: Climbing shoes.

KILLER

A really fun full-body warm-up.

Ask each climber to get into a push-up position and place a climbing shoe underneath their body.

Once everyone is in this starting position, explain to the group that they will be out of the game if their shoe is ever out of arm's reach, or if they come out of the push-up position.

The aim is for them to move around in the push-up position and steal other peoples' shoes without losing their own. The winner is the last climber remaining in the game.

WARM-UP

Group size: 4+

Equipment: None.

15. MIRROR DANCE

A good warm-up that also challenges coordination.

Ask the group to line up so that everyone is facing you, making sure that you are far enough back for them all to see you.

Explain to the group that they must copy whatever you do. For example, if you move your right leg forward, they must move their right leg forward.

Speed things up, move around quickly and make it difficult for the group to follow. For example, do a star jump, then jump into the push-up position and then onto your bottom as quickly as you can.

After 15 to 20 seconds, join the line and ask another member of the group to lead, regularly switching the leader.

WARM-UP

Group size: 8+

Equipment: None.

16. MONKEYING AROUND

This silly game is an enjoyable warm-up.

Ask the climbers to form two lines. Mark out a start and finish line about ten metres apart.

When you shout 'Go', the first climbers in the lines must race to the finish on all-fours, imitating a monkey. Repeat the race with the second, third, fourth climbers and so on.

WARM-UP

Group size: 8+

Equipment: None.

17. OBSTACLE COURSE

A really fun team-building exercise that makes a good warm-up.

Nominate one climber from the group to stand next to you.

Give the rest of the group one minute to make an obstacle course using only their bodies. They are allowed to team up, for example two people holding hands to form a circle to jump through.

Once they have created the course, ask the nominated climber to complete it.

WARM-UP

Group size: 1+

Equipment: Skipping ropes, or 4-6 metres of thin rope.

SKIPPING ROPES

In my opinion, this is one of the best pulse-raisers you can do. It also improves coordination.

If you have enough skipping ropes, simply ask the group to do one to two minutes of skipping.

Alternatively, use about four to six metres of thin rope, with someone holding each end. Start by swinging the rope, then ask a climber to jump in and skip.

Having had some time practising basic skipping, send in teams of three at a time to skip, or make things harder by adding challenges – try asking climbers to rotate every time they jump, or to skip in a squat position.

WARM-UP

Group size: 1+

Equipment: None.

STANDARD WARM-UP

A good pulse-raiser to start a session. It is useful for warming up the fingers

Ask the group to jog on the spot with their hands held out in front of them, fists clenched.

Whilst jogging, ask the climbers to point their fingers up, then close their hands again, then point fingers in towards each other, and finally back to clenched fists.

Repeat this for about 30 seconds, then shake out.

Next, ask the climbers to place their hands together but without their palms touching. Get them to push their fingers against each other, evenly at first, then applying more pressure to the index finger. Ask them to apply more pressure to individual fingers in turn, finishing with the little finger, then shake out.

WARM-UP

Group size: 2+

Equipment: None.

20. STEP WARS

An enjoyable pulse-raiser that is great for warming up the legs.

Split the group up into pairs, ask them to take off their shoes and face each other.

Explain that the objective of the game is to win points by standing on the feet of their opponent – if they manage to tap their opponent's foot then they get a point. Of course, both players are trying to touch each other's feet at the same time, making it more difficult than it sounds.

WARM-UP

Group size: 4+

Equipment: None.

21. WHEELBARROW RACE

A fun exercise and great warm-up, especially for the shoulders.

Ask the group to split into pairs and stand behind a starting line. Mark out a finishing line around eight metres from the starting line.

Climber 1 starts by getting into a push-up position. Climber 2 grabs the ankles of Climber 1, lifting them towards their armpits into a wheelbarrow position.

Explain to the group that they must race to the finish line whilst maintaining the wheelbarrow position.

After the race, swap roles and repeat.

COORDINATION DRILLS

Good coordination is such an important part of climbing, and so useful when it comes to improving people's grade, that I like to include plenty of coordination drills in each coaching session.

The majority of these drills also make great warm-ups, and regular repetition will help climbers to make progress – consider using them as part of your normal warm-up routine.

Some of these drills can be quite difficult to visualise, so it's worth testing and practising them yourself before using them in a group session.

COORDINATION DRILL

Skills: Hand-eye coordination, power, dynamic climbing.

Equipment: Beanbags.

BEANBAG CATCH CLIMBING

This drill is great for developing hand-eye coordination while training for power and dynamic climbing.

Give the climber a beanbag to hold in one hand, and ask them to choose a route of the lowest grade in the centre of the wall.

The climber gets onto the wall with one hand on the first hold, and one hand holding the beanbag. When they make the first move to the next handhold they must swap hands.

For example, let's say that their left hand is holding the beanbag, and their right hand is on the wall. When they make the first move, they must throw the beanbag into the air, catching it with their right hand as their left hand catches the next handhold.

Repeat this process, swapping hands with each move all the way up the climb.

COORDINATION DRILL

Skills: General coordination and strength.

Equipment: None.

BREAK DANCE KICK

A tricky sequence of moves when linked, but simple to break down.

Start in the push-up position with your bum slightly raised.

Step 1 – bring your right knee to your right elbow.

Step 2 – the outside of your left foot replaces your right hand, which is now just floating.

Step 3 – kick your right foot in front of you at the same time as flicking your right arm straight up.

Step 4 – hold for half a second, then begin reversing these moves, bringing your right foot and arm back into position.

Reverse all the moves until you are in the push-up position, then immediately repeat the moves on the opposite side, starting by bringing your left knee to left elbow and so on.

COORDINATION DRILL

Skills: Foot-eye coordination and deadpointing.

Equipment: None.

For a variation on this drill, check out **Deadpointing Hands** (below).

DEADPOINTING FEET

This exercise is perfect for climbers who are practising deadpointing and foot-eye coordination – important skills for dynamic climbing.

If necessary, begin by explaining that deadpointing is meeting a hold at the apex of the upward motion, when the climber has no upward or downward motion. Catching a hold at this exact time places less strain on the hold and the arm, and requires less energy to hang it.

The climber starts by getting on to the wall with both feet off the floor and their hands on two different holds. Now, without moving their hands they must move both feet to two different holds at the same time. From there, they can either jump their feet down to the starting holds, or onto two different holds, provided they move both feet simultaneously.

COORDINATION DRILL

Skills: Hand-eye coordination and deadpointing.

Equipment: None.

For a variation on this drill, check out **Deadpointing Feet** (above).

DEADPOINTING HANDS

Another exercise for climbers practising deadpointing and dynamic climbing, this time focusing on hand-eye coordination.

If necessary, begin by explaining that deadpointing is meeting a hold at the apex of the upward motion, when the climber has no upward or downward motion. Catching a hold at this exact time places less strain on the hold and the arm, and requires less energy to hang it.

The climber starts by getting onto the wall with both feet off the floor and their hands on two different holds. Now, without moving their feet, they must move their hands to two different holds at the same time. From there, they can either jump their hands back to the starting holds, or to two different holds, provided they move both hands simultaneously.

COORDINATION DRILL

Skills: Foot-eye coordination and balance.

Equipment: None.

DYNAMIC ADD-A-MOVE

This drill is perfect for developing a climber's foot-eye coordination – useful for running starts, step-step dynos and step-step kicks.

Split the group up into threes and assign each group to a slabby wall with lots of low footholds.

Climber 1 runs towards the wall and stands on a hold of their choice, before stepping back down to the ground.

Climber 2 then runs towards the wall, stands on the same hold as Climber 1, and then adds another foothold to stand on immediately after.

Climber 3 then does the same, adding a new hold to the sequence.

Repeat until the sequence gets too hard, then start again. Mix up the groups and have them try each others' challenges as well as their own.

COORDINATION DRILL

Skills: General coordination.

Equipment: Coloured tape, card, or chalk to make a grid of coloured shapes.

FLOOR DANCE

Before the session, lay out a grid of coloured shapes in a square across the floor, approximately two metres wide and two metres long. Make each grid square unique in colour or shape.

Explain to the group that they are going enter the square one at a time, and that when you shout out a command, they must jump with both feet onto the correct coloured shape.

Try shouting out a sequence of multiple colours and shapes to test the climber's coordination.

COORDINATION DRILL

Skills: General coordination, strength, power, and speed.

Equipment: None.

GERMAN TEAM ROLL

This drill is from Udo Neumann of the German National Bouldering team.

Ask the group to line up next to each other in the push-up position.

Now get the climber on the far left to roll towards the right – everyone in the push-up position must jump over the rolling climber as he passes, remaining in the push-up position as they do so.

Once the climber has rolled to the end of the line, he gets into the push-up position while the new 'far left' climber begins their roll along the line.

COORDINATION DRILL

Skills: Timing, communication and trust.

Equipment: None.

HUMAN JUMPS

This drill encourages concentration on timing and communication, and is a great trust exercise.

Split the group up into pairs, trying to match people of similar builds.

To begin the drill, Climber 1 picks up Climber 2 so that they are horizontal. Climber 1's hands should be on the outside with one hand on their partner's hip and the other on their partner's back.

Now, in a dynamic motion, Climber 1 is going to jump sidewards in the direction of Climber 2's feet, and Climber 2 needs to land on their feet. After one or two seconds, Climber 2 then jumps back, with Climber 1 landing onto their feet.

Try to repeat the exercise three or four times, keeping a dynamic flow.

COORDINATION DRILL

Skills: General coordination, strength and body tension.

Equipment: None.

CAUTION! – This exercise can be dangerous, and is best completed on a soft surface, clear of obstructions.

HUMAN TANK ROLL

This coordination drill is endless fun! It's basically a huge two-person roly-poly...

To get into the starting position, Climber 1 starts by lying on the floor facing upwards. Climber 2 stands, with their feet either side of Climber 1's head.

Climber 1 then grabs onto the ankles of Climber 2, and lifts their legs up so that Climber 2 can grab their ankles.

From this starting position, ask them to roll forward three or four times. Climber 2 is going to roll forward, pushing the feet of Climber 1 onto the floor and tucking their head in. Climber 1 keeps the momentum going with the same motion.

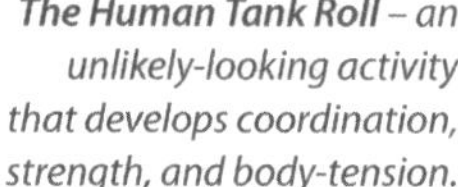

The Human Tank Roll – *an unlikely-looking activity that develops coordination, strength, and body-tension.*

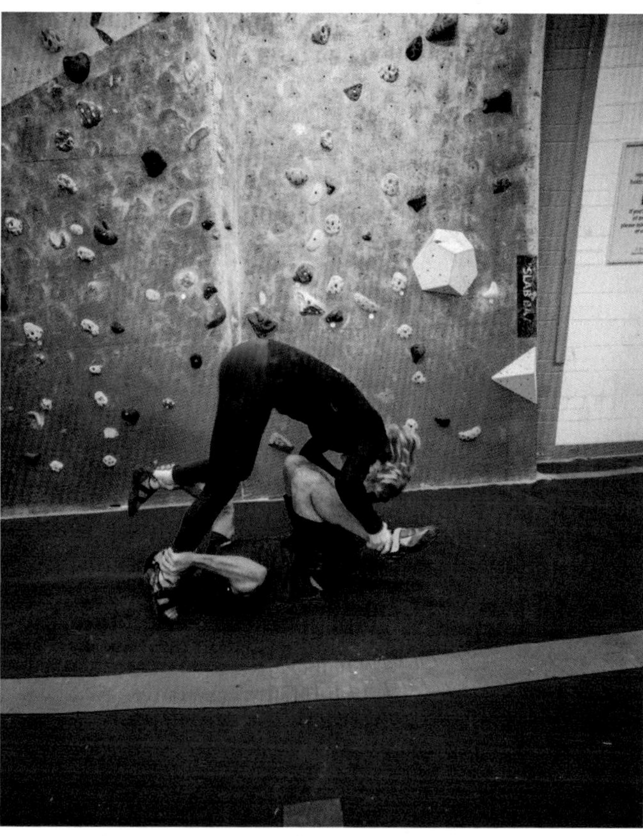

COORDINATION DRILL

Skills: Teamwork.

Equipment: None.

HUMAN TULIP

Another exercise that is great for team building.

Ask the group to split up into threes and sit in a circle with their feet in the middle.

Ask everyone to link hands and explain that they need to stand up together in one motion on your count of three.

Having done this, try the same exercise with groups of six or more – the bigger the group, the more difficult this will become.

COORDINATION DRILL

Skills: Foot-eye coordination.

Equipment: Coloured tape.

JUMP SEQUENCES

This drill is a bit confusing, but great for foot-eye coordination.

Before the session, lay out shapes on the floor using different coloured tape – I normally just do lines and crosses in three different colours. Make the pattern about four metres long by two metres wide, with a start and finish line at the ends.

Split the climbers into two groups and ask them to line up behind the start line. The first climber in the line then decides on a pattern, which his group must all copy (for example stepping on red crosses only, left foot, right foot, right foot again).

Once his group have all crossed the grid, the climber at the front of the second line chooses a pattern for his group to follow, and so on.

COORDINATION DRILL

Skills: Hand-eye coordination.

Equipment: None.

NINJA

This is more of a game than a drill, but definitely improves a climber's hand-eye timing, which is crucial for coordination.

Split the group into threes or fours and ask them to stand in a circle, holding their arms out in random directions.

Choose one person to start the game. This person must try and touch another climber's hand in one quick movement and then freeze. The other climber needs to avoid being touched by moving their hand out of the way as quickly as possible, in one movement before freezing.

If they are touched, they must put that hand behind their back and are not allowed to use it again for the rest of the game. If they manage to move it in time, they have to keep it in its new position until someone tries to touch it again.

Go around the circle, taking turns to try to touch each other's hands. Once you have both hands behind your back, you are out of the game.

COORDINATION DRILL

Skills: Coordination, memory, timing.

Equipment: None.

PUSH-UP CYCLE

This drill is great fun and really challenges coordination, memory, and timing.

Split the group into threes and ask them to line up next to each other (relatively closely) in the push-up position.

To begin the drill, the climber on the left does a push-up and then rolls rightwards towards the middle. The climber in the middle has to remain in the push-up position and jump over the climber who is rolling towards them.

The climber who has just rolled into the middle needs to get back up into the push-up position as quickly as possible, whilst the climber on the right does a push-up and rolls leftwards towards the middle.

Again, the climber now in the middle needs to jump over the rolling climber, and the climber who is now on the left can begin the sequence over again.

Encourage the climbers to perform the drill as quickly as they can.

PUSH-UP JUMP

COORDINATION DRILL

Skills: Coordination, timing.

Equipment: None.

Another drill that challenges coordination and timing.

Split the group up into pairs and ask them to spread out.

To get into position, Climber 1 starts in a forward bridge position (a push-up position with the bum raised in the air). Climber 2 begins standing nearby.

Climber 2 starts the drill by crawling through the bridge formed by his partner, and as soon as he is through, Climber 1 immediately lies down.

Climber 2 then gets up on his feet as quickly as possible, jumps over the lying-down Climber 1, and gets into the forward bridge position straight away.

Climber 1 then crawls through the bridge and continues the cycle.

Encourage the climbers to keep going as quickly as possible.

RUNNING AT VOLUMES

COORDINATION DRILL

Skills: Coordination, timing.

Equipment: None.

This is a really fun drill that improves a climber's foot-eye coordination and timing. It is also great for teaching running starts, step-step dynos and step-step kicks.

You'll need a wall with three different volumes really close to each other.

The climbers run onto the volumes, without using their hands, one after the other.

Have them start next to each other, about three metres back from the wall. Climber 1 starts on your shout of 'Go!' with the others following at about one-second intervals.

Make it harder by having the climber on the left run to the volume on the right, or all three running at the same time.

COORDINATION DRILL

Skills: Timing, hand-eye coordination.

Equipment: Beanbag.

If climbers are unfamiliar with this drill consider starting with simple throwing and catching in a circle, then practise running up the holds without the beanbag.

RUNNING STARTS TRIANGLE

This drill is perfect for improving a climber's running starts, step-step dynos, and step-step kicks. It is also great for timing, as well as foot-eye and hand-eye coordination, and is an effective pulse raiser.

Find a section of wall where it is possible to run onto three big holds or volumes, one after the other. Split the group into threes and give each group a beanbag.

The starting position is as follows:

Climber 1 stands a few metres away from the wall, holding the beanbag.

Climber 2 stands behind Climber 1.

Climber 3 stands two metres back from where the running start finishes, forming the shape of a triangle.

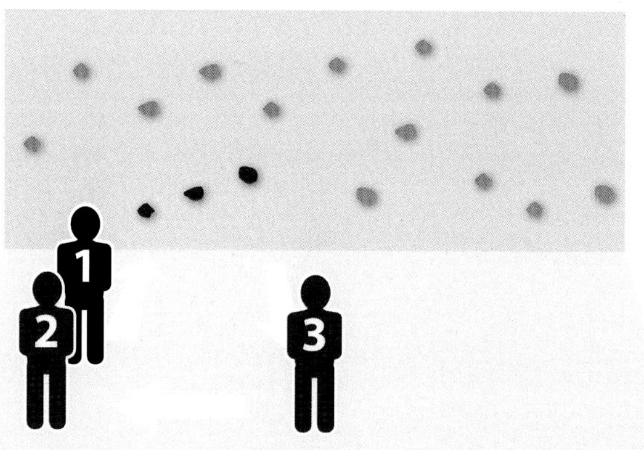

If climbers are struggling with this drill then stop and explain **running start techniques** (page 64) – talk about timing and where their eyes should be focused.

Climber 1 begins the drill by running towards the wall, and up the three footholds. Before they touch the floor, they must throw the beanbag to Climber 3, and then run to where Climber 3 is standing.

Climber 3 must catch the beanbag and immediately throw it to Climber 2, before running over to where Climber 2 is standing.

Climber 2 catches the beanbag, steps forward, and repeats the exercise. Aim to repeat the exercise three to five times without dropping the beanbag.

COORDINATION DRILL

Skills: Hand-eye coordination.

Equipment: Beanbag.

STEP AND THROW

A fun exercise to improve a climber's hand-eye coordination.

Split the climbers into groups of three and give each group a beanbag. All the climbers then get onto the wall with a gap of at least two to three metres between them.

The climber on the left starts with the beanbag and must throw it to the climber in the middle. After the middle climber has caught the beanbag, all three make one move upwards, and the climber in the middle throws the beanbag to the climber on the right. Once again, all climbers make one move upwards.

Continue this drill, passing the beanbag back and forth along the line until the climbers reach the top. You can also do this drill while down-climbing, taking a step down between each throw.

COORDINATION DRILL

Skills: Dynamic climbing, deadpointing, coordination.

Equipment: None.

This drill is traditionally used on overhangs to improve dynamic climbing and power, but also works great as a balance drill on slabby routes.

TAP AND GO

Another good drill for improving a climber's dynamic climbing, deadpointing, coordination and confidence.

Ask the climbers to climb any low-grade route of their choice. Every time they wish to use a hold with their right hand, they must first tap it with their left hand and vice versa. After they have tapped a hold, they must move their other hand to it immediately. The tapping hand is not allowed to grab any other hold until first tapped by the other hand (this effectively creates a series of one-handed dynamic moves).

If the climbers are coping well with this exercise, challenge them to perform two or three taps on a hold before they grab it.

COORDINATION DRILL

Skills: Foot-eye coordination.

Equipment: Tea towels.

TEA TOWELS

This drill is a great warm-up for the legs and hip flexors. It is also good for improving foot-eye coordination, but as with many coordination exercises it will need lots of repetition to see real improvement.

Split the group up into pairs and give each pair a tea towel. Ask both people to lift one foot off the floor.

Place the tea towel onto the first climber's lifted foot so that it is not touching the floor. Ask the climber to flick the towel to their partner, who must catch it on his foot without letting it touch the floor. Continue passing the towel back and forth in this way.

Once this drill is mastered, try the following variations:

1) Foot Swap – The person catching the towel must swap feet as the towel is flicked, catching it with their opposite foot.

2) Double Foot Swap – The person passing the towel must flick it to their opposite foot before flicking it to their partner.

"If Carlsberg did bouldering"
BLOKFEST
B
BLOKFEST.COM

CHAPTER 3

CLIMBING TECHNIQUES

Climbing is a technical sport, and making time to go climbing should always take priority over training. In this chapter we discuss a range of climbing techniques, grouped into four skill levels, along with recommended drills to help climbers work on those particular techniques.

It is recommended that climbers spend time mastering beginner techniques before moving on to novice techniques, and so on.

TECHNIQUE

Skill Level: Beginner

Recommended Drills:

Drill	Page
Bad/Good Foot Placements	70
Balance Traverse	90
Boxing Gloves	76
Feet Pulling	95
No Hands	84
Point and Go	74
Restricted Arms	101
Rounded Hands	86
Stickers Shifting	74
Weighted Feet Means Rest	88

LEGS ARE STRONGER THAN ARMS!

When asked what is the strongest part of the body, many people may be tempted to suggest the arms. In reality, of course, for most of us this is far from the case.

Imagine hanging from a hold with one arm, your legs dangling in space. If you try to pull yourself up from this position you are effectively doing a one-arm pull-up, which few people can manage. In reality, most people's arms can only lift a small percentage of their body weight.

But what about legs? If you stand on one leg with your knee bent, you can straighten it relatively easily, lifting the entire weight of your body.

This may seem very obvious now, but on the wall people have a tendency to try and pull themselves up with their arms, rather than pushing with their legs. In climbing, this should be golden rule number one – *always look down at your feet, and push with your legs rather than pulling with your arms.*

TECHNIQUE

Skill Level: Beginner

Recommended Drills:

Drill	Page
Balance Traverse	90
Boxing Gloves	76
Feet Pulling	95
Heel Hook Rockovers	96
Hover Feet	71
Hover Hands	71
No Hands	84
Point and Go	74
Pulling with Feet	101
Restricted Arms	101
Rounded Hands	86
Slab Octopus	103
Stickers Shifting	74

SHIFTING WEIGHT

Shifting weight is a fundamental technique in climbing.

If you stand with your feet shoulder-width apart, your weight is distributed evenly between both legs. Notice that your belly button is positioned centrally between both feet – this gives a good indication of the position of your centre of mass, or centre of gravity.

If you take your left leg away, without moving your hips, what will happen? A line drawn down from your centre of gravity no longer passes in between two points of contact with the ground, and as a result you will fall over. In order to successfully stand on one foot, you need to shift your entire weight onto that one foot. Where is your belly button now? You will notice that your belly button, and your centre of gravity, are directly above the weighted foot and a line drawn down to the ground must necessarily pass through that foot.

Now, standing on your right foot, you are free to move your left foot to a different hold.

Of course, on a climb, it may not always be possible to position your belly button over each foothold, and this is where hands

Warm-Ups
Coordination
Techniques
Improver Drills
Group Management
Games
Team Building
Coaching
Resources
Recommended Drills

come into the equation. It is worth remembering, however, that with your centre of gravity correctly positioned over a foothold you will be able to move to your next foothold *without* expending energy in the arms.

TECHNIQUE

Skill Level: Beginner

Recommended Drills:

Be careful not to stick your bum out, as this will load weight onto your arms instead of your feet.

STRAIGHT ARMS

It's all too easy to burn energy unnecessarily when climbing, but you can avoid doing so by hanging with straight arms as often as possible.

Imagine a monkey hanging from a branch with one arm. Almost certainly your mental image has the monkey hanging with its arm straight, as this is how monkeys successfully hang and swing in trees.

During a pull-up, when you first get onto the pull-up bar you hang with straight arms; your muscles are extended, and they expend no energy other than that required to grasp the bar, During the pull-up motion, the muscles contract, expending energy – the bit you find difficult! Even whilst holding the position at the top of the pull-up with your chin above the pull-up bar, the muscles are using energy to remain in a contracted state, before you allow them to relax back to an extended, straight arm state. When you do so, the weight is transferred to your skeleton.

In between climbing moves, it is important to focus on keeping your legs bent and your arms straight in order to minimize energy burn in your arm muscles.

TECHNIQUE

Skill Level: Beginner

Recommended Drills:

TWISTING

When climbing, it is important to have your hips close to the wall in order to keep your centre of gravity over your feet whilst keeping your arms straight.

Sometimes, footholds are positioned in a way that makes it difficult to achieve both of these things, and in this case twisting can help, particularly when only one foothold is available.

You should twist in the opposite direction to your next hold, so if you are moving your right hand, try twisting your right knee to the left, pivoting onto the outside edge of your right foot and moving your right hip close to the wall.

As you twist, you bring your right shoulder closer to your next hold, providing additional reach.

Warm-Ups | Coordination | Techniques | Improver Drills | Group Management | Games | Team Building | Coaching | Resources | Recommended Drills

TECHNIQUE

Skill Level: Novice

Recommended Drills:

BASIC FLAGGING

Flagging is the process of extending a foot in the opposite direction to your hand in order to maintain balance.

Stand on the floor with your feet shoulder-width apart, then with your left hand reach up and leftwards as far as you possibly can. What happens to your right foot? How have your hips moved? Why?

Your right foot lifts off the ground, and the right leg extends rightwards, acting as a counterbalance for your upper body as it reaches leftwards. This maintains your centre of gravity directly above your left foot, and also provides extra reach. On the rock face or climbing wall, this is what happens when we *flag*.

Imagine that you have a handhold and a foothold on your right-hand side, and your next move is to move up leftwards. When we are new to climbing, our instinct may be to lift our right foot onto that foothold because it's on our right-hand side, but when we do so we swing rightwards in an unfortunate movement known as a *barn door.*

To avoid barn-dooring, we're going to need to extend a leg in the opposite direction to that handhold up and left – ie our *right* leg. To do this, try going for that foothold out right with the outside edge of the left foot, allowing you to extend the right leg rightwards as you reach up and left with the left hand. Through some twisting and flagging, you've successfully avoided the dreaded barn door.

Choosing your boot edge – Basic flags are normally improved by placing the outside edge of your boot onto the hold.

Drawing a line – Flagging is a hard technique to master. Simply extending your leg is the easy bit, but putting it in the correct position requires a lot of attention and practice. Try drawing an imaginary line from your middle finger, through your belly button to your big toe. It should be a straight line, which means the lower your left hand is going, the higher your right foot needs to be.

Pointy toes – Always try to point your toes away from your head for optimum balance and body tension.

Pressing the foot – In most flags, pressing your foot against the wall helps to create body tension and reduces the chance of barn-dooring.

__Flagging__ – extending the right foot whilst reaching up with the left hand in order to prevent a 'barn door' to the right.

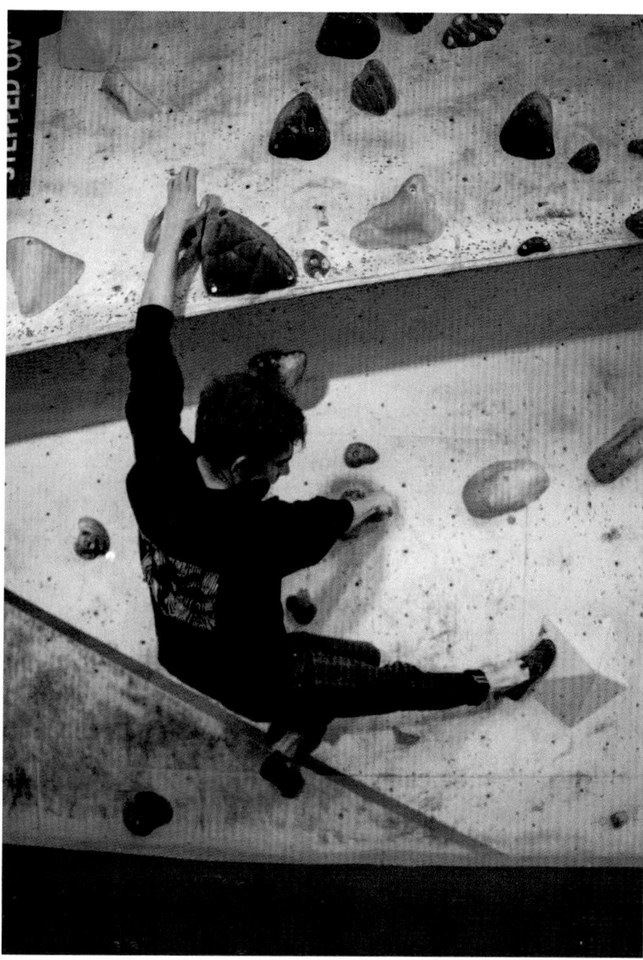

Hips into the wall – As with many climbing techniques, focus on pulling your hips into the wall with your centre of gravity directly over your weighted foot.

Lower Feet – People have a tendency to get their feet too high when flagging, causing their bum to stick out and placing more weight on their arms. Keep your feet low whenever possible.

TECHNIQUE

Skill Level: Novice

Recommended Drills:

Hover Feet	71
No Hands	71
Points Constant Ladder	118
Weighted Feet Means Rest	88
Wrong Positions	105

BRIDGING

Bridging is a technique used when climbing corners or chimneys in which you push outwards on two walls at the same time.

When climbing a corner, place a foot on each side of the corner (the technique can apply to hands as well as feet). Keeping your feet relatively wide apart enables you to gain friction on small holds or smears by pushing outwards on both walls at the same time.

This is a great technique for releasing your hands and achieving much-needed rests on hard climbs.

Bridging – Opposing pressure on two perpendicular walls releases the hands and can provide an effective rest.

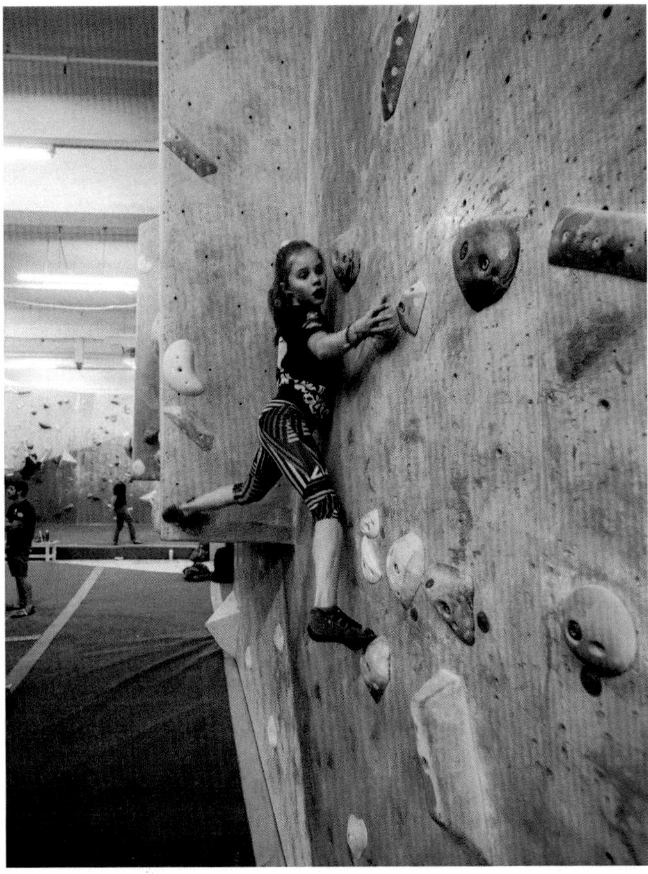

TECHNIQUE

Skill Level: Novice

Recommended Drills:

FOOT PLACEMENTS

On any climb, foot placements are crucial, but to place our feet properly takes a lot of practice.

Unless you are performing any kind of 'hook', always try to stand on your toes rather than the sole of your foot. This provides you with a large range of movement through the ankle and allows you to pivot when required.

Broadly speaking, there are three ways in which we can stand on our toes:

The front of the foot – The most obvious way to place our feet, toes pointing straight towards the wall. With the ball of the foot in contact with the rock, this can give us maximum friction on smears and slabby footholds.

The inside edge – This is the 'inside' edge of your big toe. For example the inside edge of your right foot is the left-hand side of your big toe. Inside edging still allows the foot to pivot, but lets you get your hips close to the wall.

The outside edge – Useful for getting your hips close to the wall when twisting or flagging, outside edging involves standing on your little toe.

As well as choosing which part of the foot to stand on, concentrate on deciding which part of a hold to stand on. For example, if a hold has two different edges, which one is more appropriate for a particular move?

Similarly, if it's a large hold or volume you may be tempted to put as much of your foot as possible onto the hold. However, the closer your foot is to the wall, the more you lean back and the less balance you will have. By bringing your foot back to the edge of the hold and standing on your toes, with the heel hanging off the edge, you will be able to lean in to the wall and gain balance.

Warm-Ups | Coordination | Techniques | Improver Drills | Group Management | Games | Team Building | Coaching | Resources | Recommended Drills

TECHNIQUE

Skill Level: Novice

Recommended Drills:

Drill	Page
Cork & Beanbag Elimination	77
Corks on Footholds	77
Foot Swap Every Move	70
Foot Swap on Board	113
Footwork Competition	95
Footwork Tape	80
Footwork Test	80
Hover Feet	71
Tacky Shoes	105
Technique Analysis	128

FOOT SWAPS

Quite often in climbing you are put in a situation where you have one foot where the other one needs to be. The ability and willingness to perform a foot swap is frequently the key to success on the next move.

There are several different types of foot swap, each suited to different types of hold or scenario.

The Match – This is the easiest and safest form of foot swap. It simply involves placing both feet onto the same hold in order to release one of your feet. It does, of course, rely on the hold being large enough to stand on with both feet at the same time.

The Hop – A basic foot swap that many climbers use as their standard swapping technique, in which you hop from one foot to the other. However, this is a risky foot swap which encourages bad foot placement and requires your arms to engage. Although it may be necessary in some circumstances (such as a high foothold above your centre of gravity), it is best avoided where possible.

The Tablecloth – This foot swap is less risky than the hop, enabling you to land onto your inside edge or pivot point. To perform this swap, you essentially place your free foot onto your weighted foot before quickly whipping out the weighted foot.

The Switch – This foot swap involves rolling one foot off the hold as you roll the other one onto the hold. It requires attention to detail, but is particularly useful on overhanging walls when other types of swap would increase the chance of cutting loose. To perform the swap, roll the first foot off the hold by twisting your ankle away from the wall, whilst the other foot begins a twist into the wall and onto the hold.

The Smear – This technique works best on slabs and volumes, or when the handholds are positive. Effectively, it is a method of avoiding a foot swap altogether, allowing you to place your second foot accurately onto the hold. To perform the manoeuvre, simply smear your second foot on the wall next to the hold, move your first foot to smear next to the second, then place the second foot accurately onto the hold.

Switching feet – Using a tablecloth foot swap can be less risky than a simple hop.

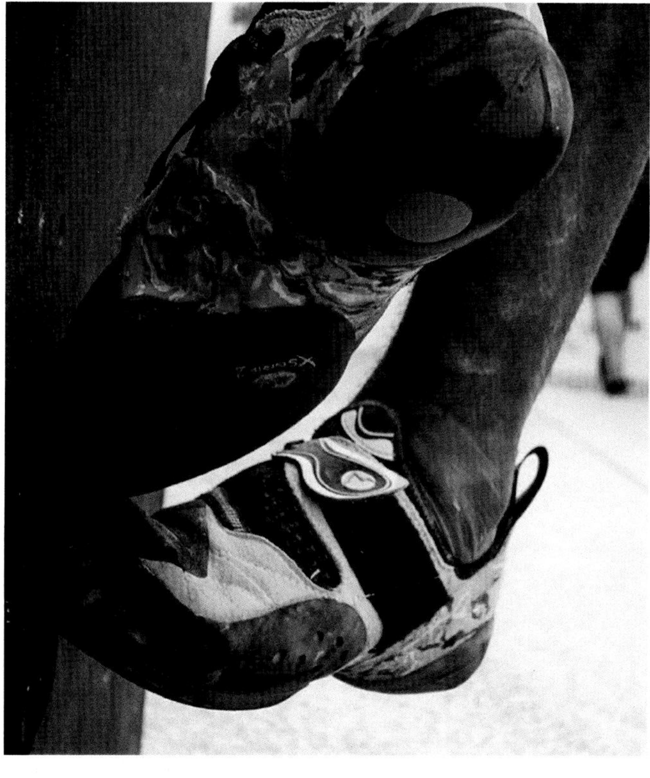

TECHNIQUE

Skill Level: Novice

Recommended Drills:

Cork & Beanbag Elimination	77
Corks on Footholds	77
No Foot Swapping	73
Smear a Foot	86
Smear, Smear, Step	86
Smear Trust	104

Try to avoid the temptation to smear too high – this makes your bum stick out and moves your centre of gravity away from your feet.

SMEARING

Smearing is the technique of using friction on the wall when there are no obvious footholds available.

To smear, place your foot against the wall with your toes pointing forward. Your knee should be bent directly over the toe in order to ensure that the force is applied directly to the point of contact – if the knee is too far forward then friction is lost and the foot will slide off. Similarly, if the knee is too far back, the heel will drop too low; again, friction will be lost.

When smearing, focus on the front of your boots and getting as much rubber as possible in contact with the wall.

Warm-Ups
Coordination
Techniques
Improver Drills
Group Management
Games
Team Building
Coaching
Resources
Recommended Drills

TECHNIQUE

Skill Level: Intermediate

Recommended Drills:

Add a Move	89
Hand Taps (Dynamic)	115
Hand Taps (Static)	115
Pointy Stick	100

DROP KNEES

A dropped knee is a type of twisting, most commonly used on overhanging climbs. It can reduce the load on your arms by pulling your centre of gravity towards the wall and over your feet.

From a position with one foothold higher than the other, twist your body towards the lower foothold, dropping the higher knee as you do so. This will pull one hip in towards the wall, keeping the centre of gravity close to the wall and over the feet. Since one shoulder is also closer to the wall, this technique will help to provide additional reach.

Although it's a simple manoeuvre in theory, remember the following points of technique:

Place the dropping foot last – Whenever possible, the foot of the knee which you intend to drop should be placed after the other foot. This will help you to gain momentum with the twist and, crucially, ensure a better placement with this foot.

Rolling the foot – The foot placement with the dropped knee is crucial, as it is going to move during the manoeuvre. You want to end up on the outside edge of your top foot, but as it isn't often possible to back-step onto the hold, you'll need to place the foot front on, or on an inside edge, and then roll the foot into the outside edge position. Be aware of the size of the hold, and make your initial foot placement to allow for this movement.

Momentum – Use the driving motion of the knee to gain consistent momentum as you roll your shoulder towards the next handhold.

Keep hips close to the wall – It is important to have your hip as close as possible to the wall, dropping the knee as far as you can. This creates body tension and enables you to take more weight off your arms.

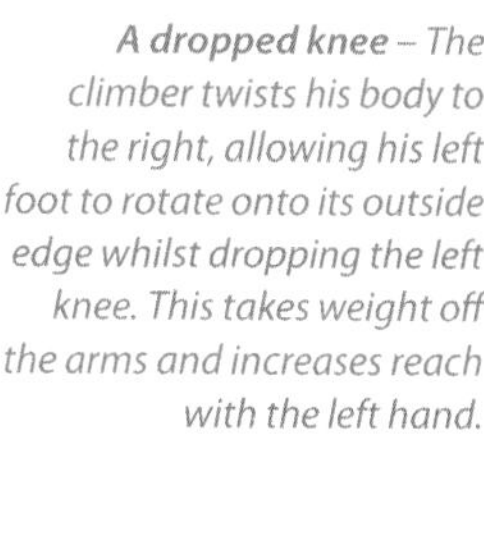

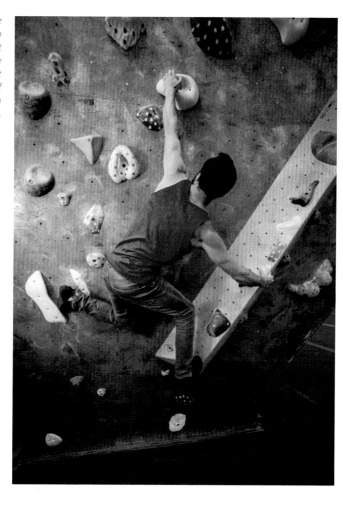

A dropped knee *– The climber twists his body to the right, allowing his left foot to rotate onto its outside edge whilst dropping the left knee. This takes weight off the arms and increases reach with the left hand.*

TECHNIQUE

Skill Level: Intermediate

Recommended Drills:

Beanbag Catch	22
Deadpointing Hands	23
Double Footed	78
Double Hand and Foot	78
Double Handed	78
Dyno Drill	93
Dyno Ladder	94
Dyno Taped	94
Dyno Time	94
Elimination	79
Golf	114
Hand Taps (Dynamic)	115
Race Game	120
Springy Climbing	87
Tap and Go	31

DYNOS

The word dyno comes from the term 'dynamic move'. It is an all-out leap that can involve zero points of contact with the wall for a short time. It is usually used when there are large distances between good holds.

A dyno – The climber leaps upwards to reach a far-away hold.

***Shifting weight* –** The technique of shifting weight has been described earlier in this chapter and plays an important role in dynamic climbing – particularly when you have one foothold higher than the other.

When faced with a dyno, many climbers will try to draw a line by jumping diagonally from the starting position to the finishing position. Instead, focus on drawing two lines – the first one shifts your weight onto the higher foot before the upward motion really begins. This enables you to generate maximum power from the legs, which are far stronger than your arms.

Momentum – Momentum is important in any dynamic move, and it can be useful to 'swing' in order to generate this momentum. However, never do more than one swing – to do so will tire your arms without providing additional momentum.

Begin by hanging as low as you can on your starting holds, arms fully extended and legs bent. Push with your legs so that your body is as high as it can be without leaving the starting holds. Next, allow yourself to drop down (or swing back) into the starting position.

Immediately, and with explosive power, push with your legs and arms to propel your centre of gravity towards the holds you are aiming for.

Head flick – Using your head in climbing, at least in a literal and physical sense, is a strange and difficult concept to grasp. In this case, however, it can make a huge difference to the distance gained in a dyno.

The average adult head weighs approximately 5kg (10 to 11 pounds), and by flicking your head in the direction of the dyno you will gain significant momentum. To do this, you should look towards the hold you are aiming for during the first stage of your 'momentum swing'. During step two, look down. Then, as you begin step three, the launching phase, flick your head up in the direction of the dyno.

TECHNIQUE

Skill Level: Intermediate

Recommended Drills:

Flagging Line 81
Flag Happy 81
No Foot Swapping 73
Tech Flags Only 129

FLAGGING – BACK FLAGS

Back flagging is a method of flagging that can remove the need for a foot swap – useful if a swap is not possible, or to conserve energy.

Basic flagging is described on page 38. When performing a back flag, the same principles apply – you still flag your leg in the opposite direction to your hand, and can still draw a direct line from hand to foot through your belly button. When back flagging, however, the free leg is extended behind the weighted leg. It is usually used when the foothold is higher than knee-height.

To perform the back flag, stand on the inside edge of your weighted foot. If you were to stand on the outside edge, or with toes pointing forward, your weight would be forced outwards with your centre of gravity no longer over your feet.

Keep the weighted leg bent, extending the free leg behind it. Just as with basic flagging, it is still important to imagine a line from your middle finger through your belly button to your big toe. Your toes, again, should be pointed away from the head.

Pushing the outside edge of the flagging foot into the wall will provide better tension and help to keep your body close to the wall. Focus on pulling your hips into the wall and keeping your weight as directly over your feet as possible – your belly button should be above your weighted foot.

TECHNIQUE

Skill Level: Intermediate

Recommended Drills:

Flagging Line 81
Flag Happy 81
No Foot Swapping 73
Tech Flags Only 129

FLAGGING – INSIDE FLAGS

Just like the back flag, an inside flag can be used to avoid the need for a foot swap. This time it is used when you have a low foothold.

To perform the inside flag, stand on the inside edge of your weighted foot and pass your free leg in front of your weighted leg so that it is between the weighted leg and the wall.

Inside flags work best when your weighted leg is straight, so they are best used on low footholds. This ensures that your weight is over the weighted foot and allows you to manoeuvre the free leg between the wall and your body.

As with all flags, you should still concentrate on achieving a straight line between your middle finger through your belly button to your big toe, whilst pointing your toes away from your head. As usual, pushing the flagging foot against the wall will create body tension and help to keep your weight close to the wall.

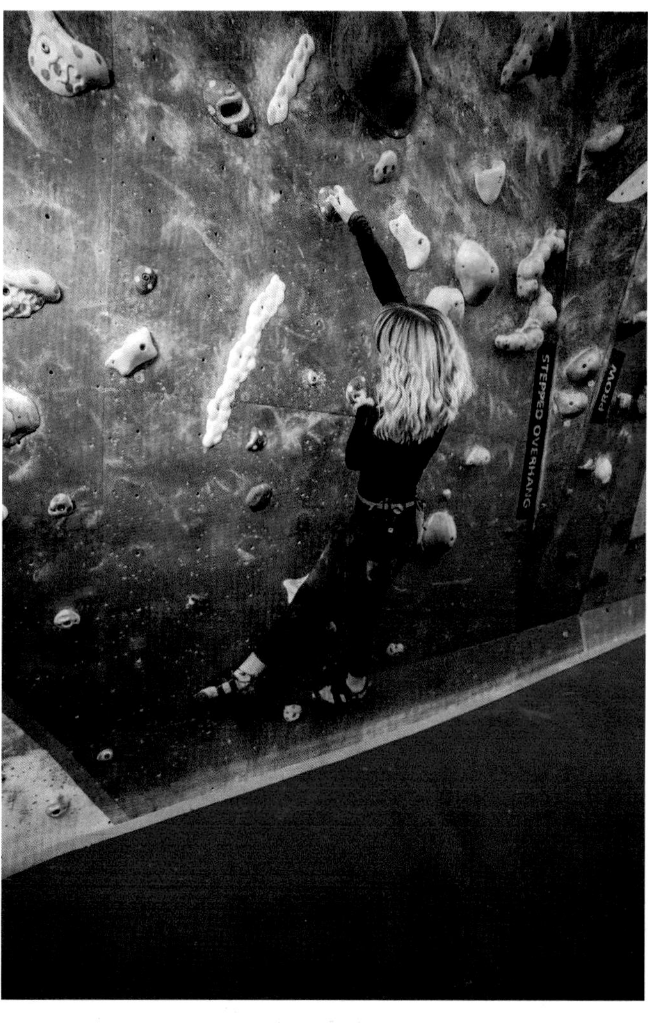

An inside flag *– Passing the free foot in front of the weighted foot allows the climber to move leftwards without needing to swap feet.*

TECHNIQUE

Skill Level: Intermediate

Recommended Drills:

Avoid the Cut	108
Dizzy Climbing	112
Heel Hook Rockovers	96
Heel Starts	97
Heel to Hand	82
Roof Heel Toe Match	123
Roof Hooking	123

HEEL HOOKS

A heel hook makes use of the heel of the shoe, rather than the toes, usually to pull you into the wall or maintain a certain body position.

Heel hooks use a pulling motion with our largest muscle groups, which are more usually used for pushing. This pulling motion engages the hamstring and glutes, and can bring your hips closer to the wall and take weight off your arms.

Deciding when to use a heel hook can be tricky, but a rule of thumb is to use the heel on holds which are higher than your belly button, and to use your toes on those holds that are lower. Using toes on very high holds pushes your body out from the wall and requires arm strength to pull your weight up and over the hold. When a heel is used in this situation, you are able to pull your weight up over the hold using the much larger leg muscles.

When performing a heel hook, it is important to point your

__A heel hook__ – Used on a high foothold, the heel hook helps to keep the climber's weight close to the wall and allows him to use powerful leg muscles for the next move.

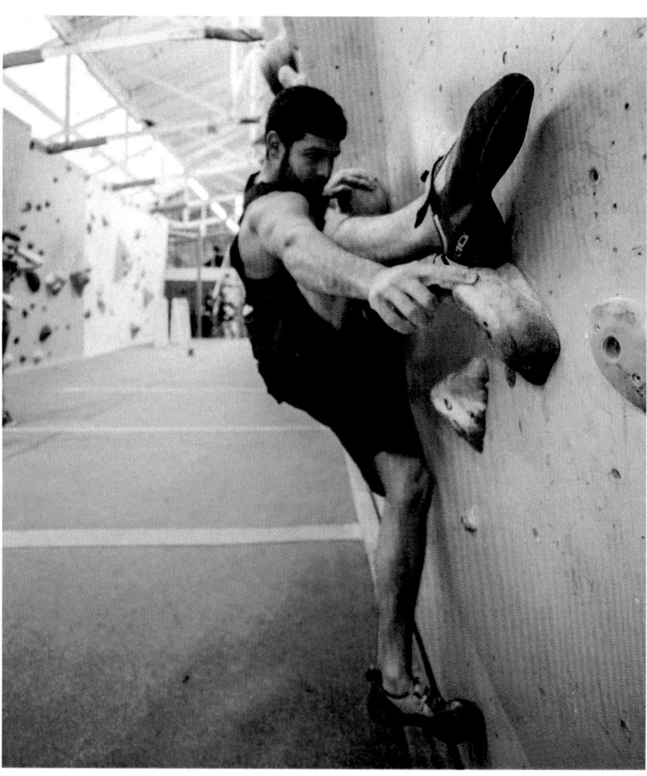

toes away from your head. This will tense up the calf muscle, creating tension and applying pressure to the hold. This can be demonstrated through a simple exercise – try sitting on the floor with your leg out in front of you and your toes relaxed. Feel your calf muscle. Next, point your toes away from your head and notice how the calf muscle tenses up. When performing the heel hook, this tension in the calf muscle is what pulls you in towards the wall.

Be sure to point your toe as soon as the heel hook is placed, and continue applying pressure for the duration of the heel hook. Bear in mind that as you point your toe, your heel will roll and move slightly on the hold – this fact should be considered when choosing the initial heel placement.

Types of heel hook – Heel hooks can be considered in two main types: the normal heel and the side heel. The normal heel hook is where you place the ball of the heel onto the hold – this is particularly useful when traversing or moving sidewards as it enables you to hang on your leg and rest your arms. The side heel, on the other hand, is better for maintaining momentum when moving straight upwards. Placing the outside of the heel onto the hold, with the sole facing the wall, can generate upwards momentum without pulling you sidewards.

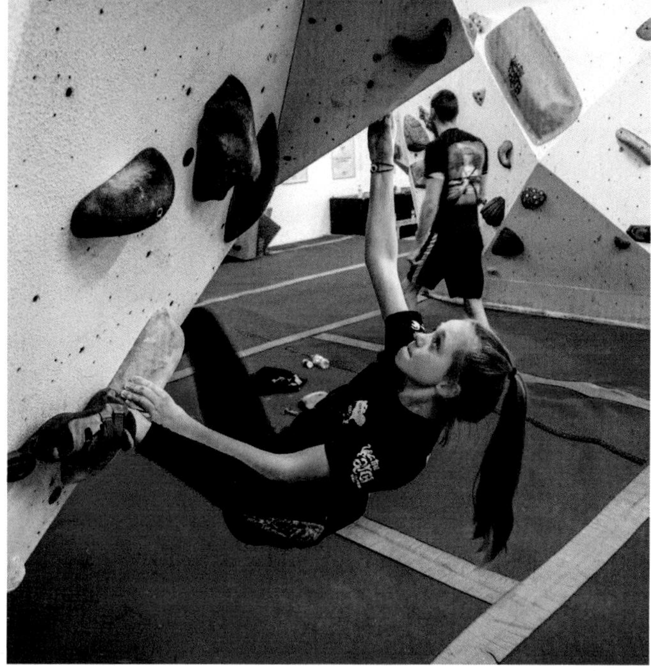

A side heel *– By placing the outside of the heel onto the hold with the sole of the foot facing the wall, the climber generates upwards momentum without pulling herself leftwards.*

Warm-Ups | Coordination | Techniques | Improver Drills | Group Management | Games | Team Building | Coaching | Resources | Recommended Drills

TECHNIQUE

Skill Level: Intermediate

Recommended Drills:

MANTLES

A common technique when topping out or climbing slabs, a mantle (or mantle-shelf) is the manoeuvre that you would use to get out of a swimming pool without using the ladder – pushing down with the arms until it is possible to lift a foot up to the level of the hands.

During a mantle you will need to lean into the wall and flip one (or both) of your elbows so they are pointing upwards. Then, push downwards until you are as high as possible before raising a foot. If you are going to flip both elbows upwards, then always try to do it one at a time, usually starting with the one on the side to which you'll raise a foot.

In the case of two hands on the top (or ledge) onto which you are going to mantle, but no footholds, always try to smear your feet as high as possible until you can get one foot over the top. In this case it may help to use a heel, allowing you to pull up with your main leg muscles.

TECHNIQUE

Skill Level: Intermediate

Recommended Drills:

PALMING

Palming, as you can probably guess from the name, involves using the palm of your hand. This can be a great way of conserving energy, as by pushing instead of pulling we work an entirely different muscle group.

Palming is normally used when slab climbing, but can also be used on vertical walls, corners, and chimneys, when there isn't a handhold available. The technique relies solely on friction between your hand and the wall.

Place the palm of your open hand against the flat wall, pushing with the heel of your palm, rather than the fingers. Focus on pointing your fingers either to the side or straight downwards in order to ensure downward pressure through the palm.

TECHNIQUE

Skill Level: Intermediate

Recommended Drills:

ROCKOVERS

Normally used on slabs or vertical walls, a rockover occurs when you have a high foothold and you need to transfer your weight up and over the hold. The technique is sometimes combined with a heel hook.

When performing a rockover, you are aiming to end up with your centre of gravity over the high foothold – think about moving up to position your belly button directly above your weighted foot. This is a harder and exaggerated version of shifting weight, but the principles of drawing two lines still apply. Shift the weight onto the high foot first, before moving up the wall.

During the move, focus on driving with your knee and pulling your hips in towards the wall, aiming to position your centre of gravity over the hold as quickly as you can.

A rockover onto a large, high foothold – *This is a two-stage manoeuvre in which the climber transfers her weight onto the foothold before using her leg muscles to move upwards.*

Drive the knee – It is helpful to push the knee as far over as possible in order to pull your weight across and over the hold.

Pull your hips in towards the wall – This helps you to take weight off your arms and position your centre of gravity over the foothold.

Concentrate on the flagging leg – A common mistake is to focus entirely on the high foot, but it is the position of the other, unweighted leg that is often the problem in unsuccessful rockovers. Depending on the geometry of the move, you will need to flag with your other foot in order to position your centre of gravity over the foothold. During the move, concentrate on the flagging leg and position it to improve your balance.

Pull with the foot – Focus on pulling your weight onto the foothold using your foot, instead of relying on your arms.

TECHNIQUE

Skill Level: Intermediate

Recommended Drills:

TOE HOOKS

A toe hook is similar to a heel hook in that it involves a pulling motion. This time, however, your leg is normally straight and you use the hook to hold your weight rather than pulling yourself towards a hold.

Toe hooks give you balance and leverage to make progress, particularly when climbing steep overhangs and roofs. Sometimes it is possible to get a toe hook on a large hold where your hand is, in order to hold your weight and release your hand without cutting loose. At other times, toe hooks can be useful on arêtes, side-pulls and undercuts.

When toe hooking, use the top part of your toes and flex your foot, pointing your toes towards your head. This will engage the calf muscle and provide body tension.

When to use a toe hook – Toe hooks are best utilised when there is a large hold facing away from you. An example of this is a jug that is facing the wrong way, far enough away from your body that your leg can be kept completely or nearly straight.

Pulled toes – Unlike in the majority of climbing techniques, your toes should be pointed towards your head. This engages the calf muscles and helps to hold tension in your body, keeping constant pressure on the foothold.

Legs straight – Toe hooks become harder the closer they are to your body. Focus on trying to extend your legs as much as possible, using your hips to pull away from the foothold.

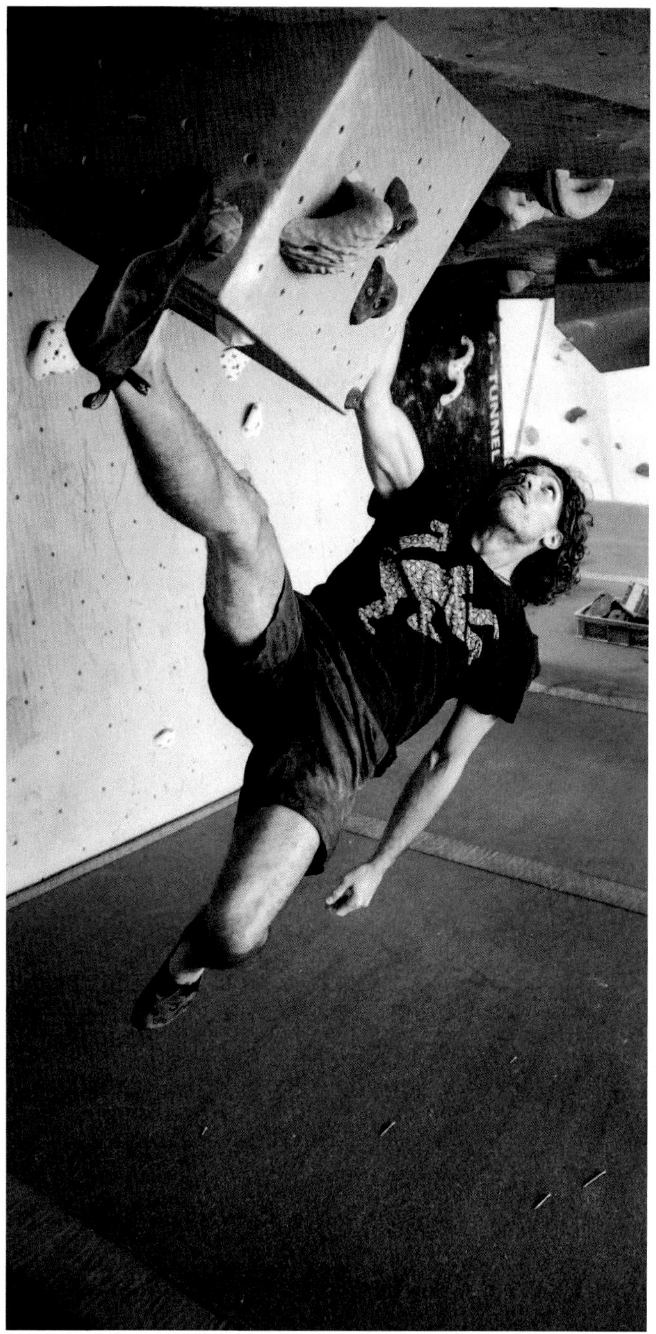

A toe hook *– With the leg almost straight, the climber is able to take lots of weight off his arms and generate good body tension.*

TECHNIQUE

Skill Level: Advanced

Recommended Drills:

BREATHING

Considering that we do this over twenty thousand times a day, it's amazing how often we forget to do it whilst climbing. Breathing delivers vital oxygen to our muscles – forgetting to breathe means we get more tired, more quickly.

Try to develop the habit of taking a few deep breaths before and after each climb, as well as remembering to breathe whenever you can during the climb.

Breathing out is also a beneficial trick in certain strenuous moves, similar to breathing out during the hard part of a push-up. Exhaling tenses your core and increases your body tension; you can feel this by placing a finger on your stomach and exhaling rapidly.

An example in climbing would be exhaling as you latch a hold that you've popped for – doing so will engage your core and provide you with extra tension that can help you hang the hold. Exhaling is also important when cutting loose, and during campus moves and roof climbing.

TECHNIQUE

Skill Level: Advanced

Recommended Drills:

CAMPUSING

The term campusing is used in climbing when you make a move with your hands whilst your legs are hanging free, not touching the wall – just like if you were swinging around on monkey bars.

Campusing is extremely strenuous and is normally only used when climbing a roof or an overhanging wall. In some cases it can be used to avoid huge swings and therefore save energy on hard moves. To be effective in this way, it requires good technique.

Knees up **–** Bringing your knees up as you start the move will generate momentum and make the move easier. This also reduces the large pendulum effect created by your legs, and effectively reduces the weight that your arms must carry.

Gaining momentum **–** This technique goes hand-in-hand with lifting the knees. On huge campus moves, gaining and maintaining momentum is essential. Start off by using your arms to pull your weight up as if doing a pull-up. From here, straighten your arms again and then pull immediately through the pull-up position towards your next hold.

Exhale as you go **–** Breathe out as you perform the pull-through motion and grab your next hold. This breathing will tense your core, increase your body tension and help to reduce the pendulum as you latch the hold.

Campusing – Although an inherently strenuous manoeuvre, a campus move can sometimes be the best option as it avoids a large swing. This moves requires both strength and good technique to be effective.

TECHNIQUE

Skill Level: Advanced

Recommended Drills:

THE CAMPUS SWING

A campus swing is a more technical and less strenuous version of campusing.

It involves swinging your hips and legs from side to side to gain momentum, enabling you to campus without bending your arms. This saves energy and provides additional distance.

Imagine you are hanging on a big hold in a caved area, and the next hold is too far to reach by pulling through and campusing. You can generate momentum by swinging your legs away from the next hold. Allow yourself to swing back and forth, drawing a line between your current handhold and the next one. After approximately three swings, your legs should have generated enough momentum – now, as they swing towards your next hold, let go with one hand and let the swing bring you towards the next hold.

The timing of when to let go is crucial here, so experiment to see what works best. Normally, letting go as soon as your legs are coming past your current hold is a good rule of thumb. Once you have let go, it will feel natural to try to bend your arms; to do so will instantly kill the swing and force you to start over again.

Swing direction **–** Be sure that the axis of your swing is in line with the hold you are aiming for.

Straight arms **–** Keep your arms straight throughout the swing. Bending your arms will not only be tiring, but will lose any momentum that you have gained.

Timing **–** This requires coordination, experimentation and practice. Try to let go as your legs come past your hands on the final swing. If you let go too early or too late then you are likely to swing off the hold.

Other techniques **–** Understand how using your hips will help with other techniques, and how you can include it in both general dynamic climbing, and even static moves such as rockovers.

TECHNIQUE

Skill Level: Advanced

Recommended Drills:

CUTTING LOOSE

The term 'cutting loose' is given to a move in which both feet come completely off the wall. Although frequently associated with bad technique, it is sometimes a necessity to make progress on a hard climb.

Cutting loose obviously puts a lot of strain on your arms and will drain energy and strength. To minimise this loss, it is important to cut loose in a controlled fashion – this could be the difference between holding a big 'cut loose' or not.

When your legs swing away from the wall they create a huge pendulum which may prevent you from staying on the wall. It is therefore necessary to absorb as much energy as possible by reducing this pendulum. To do this, tuck your elbows in with bent arms. At the same time, tense your core and bring your knees towards your chest.

Bent arms – It is very important to keep your arms bent. Not only does this pre-contract the muscles, but it also gives you extra time to absorb the impact of the swing. Straight arms increase the length of the pendulum and are likely to be ripped straight off their holds.

Elbows tucked in – Inexperienced climbers will often have their elbows pointing outwards, isolating the biceps. Instead, tuck the elbows in to engage the *latissimus dorsi* – one of the main muscles used in climbing.

Knees up – As you cut loose, bring your knees up. This reduces the length of the pendulum and engages your core.

Cutting loose – Whilst commonly associated with bad climbing technique, cutting loose is sometimes a necessary evil. Keeping your elbows tucked in, with the arms and knees bent will reduce the likelihood of swinging off your holds.

TECHNIQUE

Skill Level: Advanced

Recommended Drills:

Drill	Page
Dynamic Smear Push Drill	113
Dyno Drill	93
Dyno Ladder	94
Dyno Time	94
Speed Climbing	87

DYNAMIC FOOT SMEAR

A dynamic foot smear can be used when performing a big dynamic move that isn't a full dyno.

The technique involves hopping the foot that you would naturally flag with onto the wall, then pushing off the smear. This generates momentum and provides a lot more reach.

For example, if you are going up to your left and you have a left foothold, it feels normal to pull up and perform a 'mini rockover'. A dynamic foot smear turns this otherwise static rockover-type move into more of a speedy pop, using momentum to gain height and distance.

Try to deliver the move in one step – pop your foot up in the direction where you would normally flag, but have your foot higher up so your knee is bent. As it lands on the wall, bend the knee, then extend it immediately to generate push and momentum. Aim to treat it as one move so you don't end up waiting in the bent knee position.

TECHNIQUE

Skill Level: Advanced

Recommended Drills:

Drill	Page
Boxing Gloves	76
Corks on Footholds	77
Feet Pulling	95
Footwork Competition	95
Footwork Tape	80
Footwork Test	80
Pivoting a Foot	99
Roof Pinning	124
Stab and Go	104
Sticky Eyes	87
Technique Analysis	128

PULLING IN WITH FEET

Experiment with this next time you go climbing. Make up a really simple and easy rockover, with two juggy handholds and a foothold up and right.

Begin by hanging on the jugs, both arms straight, with two smears directly underneath you. Next, place your right foot onto the foothold and begin to rockover.

You will notice that it feels natural to pull in with your arms to at least 90 degrees, then shift your weight over the foot by pushing with your arms. In doing this, you are using your lats and biceps to pull yourself close to the wall, then the opposing muscle groups (triceps and shoulders) to push your centre of gravity over your foot.

As we know, however, it is best to use our legs and core as much as possible, rather than just our arms, and this move is no exception – try to use your footholds as mini handholds.

Imagine placing a stick on the floor and dragging it towards you with your foot. As you do so, you carry out a process called pinning, and will engage your glutes, core, and legs. Now try this on the rockover, focusing on pulling the foothold towards you

When placing your feet, try to get into the habit of thinking about how you can pull with them. For example, if using a triangular hold, try to place your toe over the point of the triangle so that you can get some 'pull' from it, rather than just pushing off the flat face.

with your toes. Try to end up with your belly button over your foot as you normally would, but resist pulling in with your arms at all. If you use your feet and core correctly, it should be possible to perform the rockover with your arms completely straight.

Pulling in with the feet is an important technique and should be used whenever possible. In doing so we take a lot of weight off our arms, and save energy.

TECHNIQUE

Skill Level: Advanced

Recommended Drills:

ROUTE READING

Being able to 'read' a route is an important skill in climbing, and one you will gain naturally with experience.

Jumping straight onto a route without a prior look can waste huge amounts of energy and potentially cost you that all-important first attempt.

Take time to note where certain holds are, as you may not be able to see them once you are on the wall. Pay particular attention to holds around corners or beneath larger holds or overhangs.

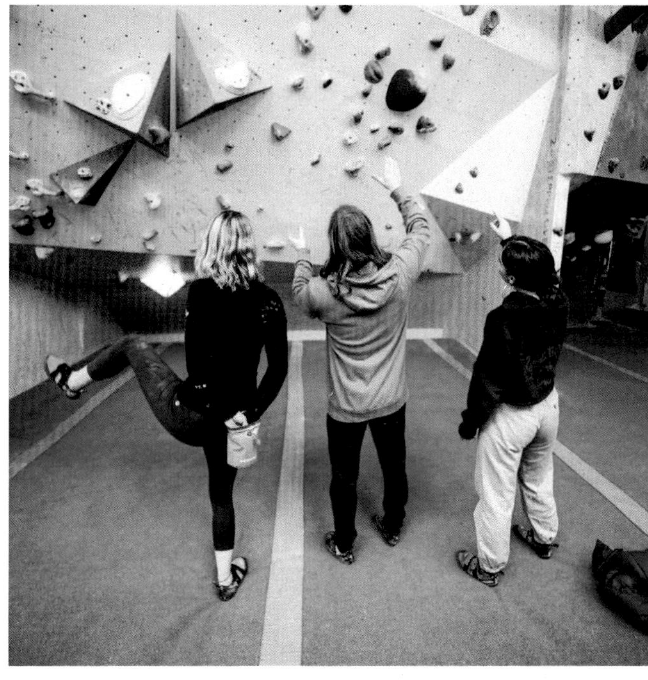

Route reading – Taking the time to 'read' a route before you start can make the difference between success and failure.

Another thing to consider is the sequence in which you will move your hands – it might be crucial to arrive with a particular hand on a certain hold.

Making route reading a habit before you start climbing will benefit you in endless ways and help you save energy once on the wall.

TECHNIQUE

Skill Level: Advanced

SCARY MOVES – BAT HANGS

The bat hang consists of a double toe hook, holding you in position and giving you balance and leverage. In some cases, you are able to let go entirely with your hands and take a rest.

Bat hangs are, of course, most useful on roofs and overhangs; you'll need a large positive hold that is facing away from you, and big enough to fit both feet onto. An example would be a jug facing the wrong way, far enough from your body that your legs will be straight or nearly straight.

When using the bat hang, focus on using the top part of your toes, and flexing your foot so that the toes are pointing towards your head. As with the toe hook, it's important to keep the legs as straight as possible.

Bat hangs are a crucial part of roof climbing in the higher grades, but as you might expect, the techniques are similar to those of the toe hook:

Pulled toes – Unlike most climbing techniques, avoid the 'pointy toes' style and pull your toes towards your head. This will engage your calf muscles and help to hold tension in your body.

Legs straight – Bat hangs become harder the closer you are to the hold that you're trying to hang from. Focus on trying to extend your legs as much as possible to optimise the toe hooks.

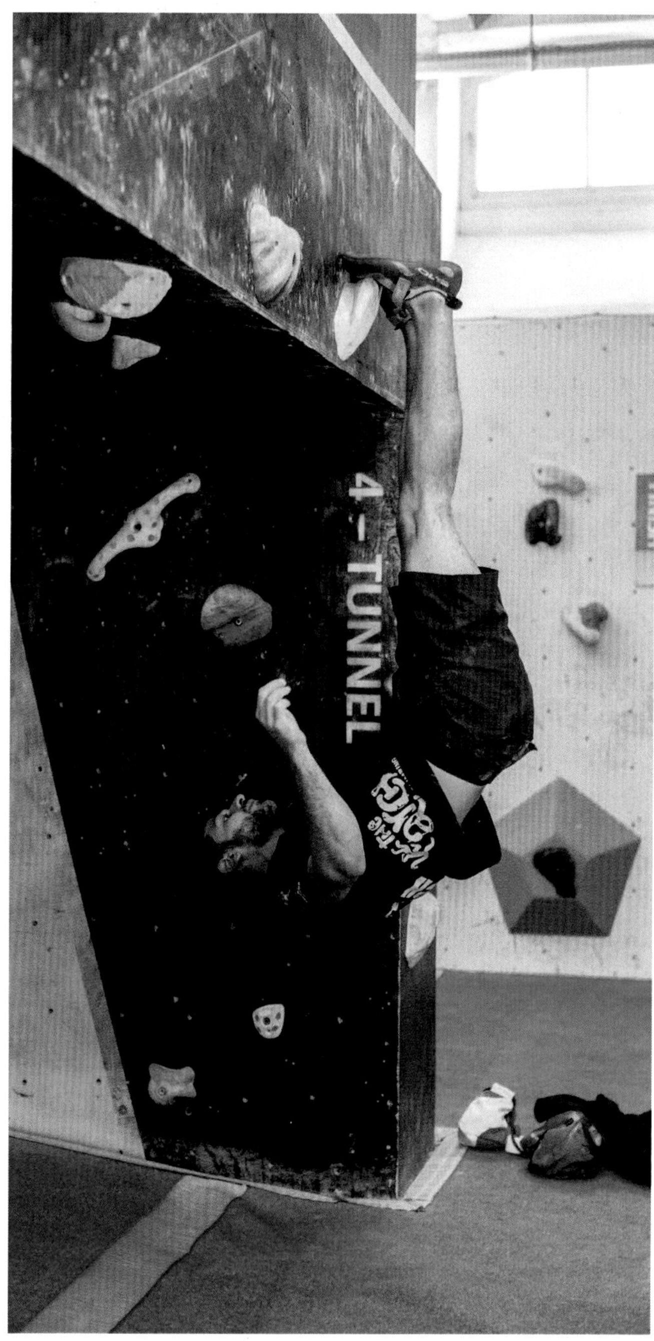

***The bat hang** – In some cases it may be possible to completely release the hands in order to take a rest.*

TECHNIQUE

Skill Level: Advanced

SCARY MOVES – KNEE BARS

Although frequently used outdoors, this move is rare at the climbing wall. It involves placing your foot against a hold whilst pressing your knee against another large feature or hold.

In some cases, this stylish move enables you to hold your entire weight with your knee to the extent that you can actually let go with both hands for a rest.

To perform the knee bar, place your foot onto a hold, then slide your knee across the feature until it cams. With harder knee bars you will need to push with your toes to keep your knee in position, which requires strong calf muscles.

TECHNIQUE

Skill Level: Advanced

Recommended Drills:

Beanbag Catch Climb 22
Deadpointing Feet 23
Deadpointing Hands 23
Dynamic Add a Move 24
Dyno Drill 93
Dyno Ladder 94
Dyno Taped 94
Dyno Time 94
Jump Sequences 27
Running at Volumes 29
Running Starts Triangle 30
Speed Climbing 87
Tap and Go 31

SCARY MOVES – RUNNING STARTS

Sometimes, especially in indoor climbing, the first handhold is way above your maximum reach. In these situations, the only way to reach the hold may be with a running start.

This is exactly as it sounds, and involves running towards the wall and using either an initial foothold or a smear to reach the first handhold.

It is important to keep a consistent speed during the run-up without any hesitation. A bad habit is to run towards the wall, but slow down just before you reach the wall, losing your momentum.

Try to keep your eye on the initial foothold rather than the hold that you are jumping to. Failing to do so can result in you running into the wall. Avoid the temptation to look up towards your handhold before your foot lands on the foothold.

Finally, as with a big dyno, focus on trying to flick your head towards your handhold as you jump, providing you with extra momentum.

TECHNIQUE

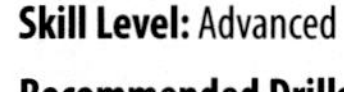

Skill Level: Advanced

Recommended Drills:

SCARY MOVES – STEP-STEP DYNOS

A step-step dyno is basically a running start, but with two or more steps. Imagine a running start that requires you to run onto a foothold, and then onto another foothold before jumping up to the first handhold – this is a step-step dyno.

As with a running start, it is important to keep a consistent speed during the run-up, and to keep your eyes on the footholds rather than the hold you are jumping to.

The following techniques apply to both running starts and step-step dynos:

Keep your eyes on the foothold – It's very natural when running towards the wall to look up at the hold you are jumping to, causing you to miss the foothold. It is crucial to keep your eye on the foothold until your foot is on it. You can incorporate the head flick as your foot lands on the hold to gain some extra height.

When I'm coaching this technique, people normally respond by saying, 'But then I don't know where I'm jumping to'. In reality, however, we have incredible spatial awareness; if we learn to trust our senses then we do not need to keep our eyes fixed on something to know where it is.

Pick an object that you can currently see, look at it, and then close your eyes. Now point to the object with your eyes shut, and then open your eyes. You will notice that you are pointing directly towards the object. This principle applies equally well to the hold you are jumping for.

One motion – Generating momentum is key. A bad habit, normally caused by a lack of commitment, is to change the pace and slow down as you reach the foothold. Instead, keep the speed consistent and treat the entire move as one motion.

Smearing – Don't get fixated on the only holds available. Quite often it is easier to smear than to aim for a poorly positioned hold.

Speed followed by control – Once your foot is planted on the initial hold, slow down to a more controlled pace – you normally have more time than you think, and should control your momentum so as not to 'overshoot'.

TECHNIQUE

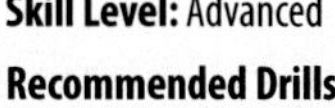

Skill Level: Advanced

Recommended Drills:

Beanbag Catch Climb	22
Deadpointing Feet	23
Deadpointing Hands	23
Dynamic Add a Move	24
Dyno Drill	93
Dyno Ladder	94
Dyno Taped	94
Dyno Time	94
Jump Sequences	27
Running at Volumes	29
Running Starts Triangle	30
Speed Climbing	87
Tap and Go	31

SCARY MOVES – STEP-STEP KICKS

Very similar to a step-step dyno, the step-step kick finishes with a rapid foot swap, followed by a flag to stop the swing.

Imagine doing a step-step dyno that leads up and right. You go left foot first, and then right foot. When you latch the handhold, your left leg is barn-dooring you off the wall; if the handhold is poor then you may not be able to hold on. As we know from our flagging experience, we can help by kicking a foot out in the opposite direction for balance.

To do this we must perform a quick foot swap and kick our other leg out to the right. Sometimes, instead of flagging, there will be a foothold to aim for.

Bear in mind that this all happens in the space of a second or two, and will require a lot of coordination and accuracy. Quite often, moves like this require some trial and error to get the correct muscle memory; before you go for the move on the wall, it can help to replicate the sequence on the floor.

TECHNIQUE

Skill Level: Advanced

Recommended Drills:

Point and Go	74
Straight Arm Campus	126
Windmill Drill	129

WINDMILLS

A windmill is using your arm to either create momentum, gain balance, or weight a hold correctly.

Generally in climbing we release handholds by letting go of the hold and moving our hand straight up. Sometimes, however, it is necessary to drop our hand down towards the floor first in order to weight a hold correctly.

An example of this is when trying to match on a poor sloper. Instead of trying to pull or hold our weight with the one arm remaining on the wall, we can drop into the hold and use our back muscles to take the weight. This is obviously a far stronger muscle group than the arms.

Another form of windmill is used when performing a large rockover. In this case you release your arm out in a semi-circle, starting low and coming all the way up and away from your body, before rising up above you. This can help generate momentum, whilst also keeping you in balance. By bringing your arm down and around your body, you are able to keep your body close to the wall.

KENT &
TEAM
MALE
19
FEMALE
19
JUNIOR BOYS
19
JUNIOR GIRLS
19

CHAPTER 4
IMPROVER DRILLS

This chapter suggests a variety of exercises or drills designed to improve a climber's performance. Some of these drills are specific to a certain technique, whilst many cover and improve a wide range of techniques at the same time. Others have both a technique and training focus.

The exercises are arranged by skill level, from *beginner* drills through to *novice*, *intermediate*, and *advanced* level exercises. This is, of course, at the discretion of the coach and climber, and variations will make most of these drills easier or more difficult as required.

IMPROVER DRILL

Skill Level: Beginner

Group Size: 1-20

GOOD & BAD PLACEMENTS

This is a really good drill for beginners learning about footwork.

Ask the climber to climb three different routes. On their first go they should climb using the worst part of their shoes, making deliberately bad foot placements.

Afterwards, ask them to climb the same three routes using the best possible part of their shoes.

Call them in and discuss which parts of the shoes were useful, and why. Also elicit which parts of the shoes made the exercise more difficult, and why we should avoid using those parts when climbing.

IMPROVER DRILL

Skill Level: Beginner

Group Size: 1-12

BEANBAG ON HEADS

This exercise is perfect for younger climbers who are still building confidence and learning their range of movement. It also encourages route reading, shifting weight, static climbing and much more.

Ask the climbers to choose an easy traverse or an easy climb.

Give each climber a beanbag, which they must put on their head. They have to climb the entire route without dropping the beanbag.

This activity also works well in pairs, with the second person making sure the climber is not cheating. They can also give advice on footholds, since the climber can't look down.

IMPROVER DRILL

Skill Level: Beginner

Group Size: 1-20

For a variation to this drill, try combining it with **No Matching Drill** (page 73).

FOOT SWAP EVERY MOVE

This exercise is great for climbers who are practising their foot swapping skills.

Ask the climbers to climb a route about 2 grades below their hardest grade. They must perform a foot swap of their choice on every foothold they touch.

IMPROVER DRILL

Skill Level: Beginner

Group Size: 1-20

For a variation on this drill, try combining it with **Hover Hands** (page 71). It also works well in the same session as **Sticky Eyes** (page 87).

HOVER FEET

This exercise is perfect for climbers who are practising their footwork. It is also a great drill when trying to encourage climbers to climb with quiet feet.

Ask the climbers to choose a route to climb. Every time they wish to move a foot, they have to hover their foot about an inch away from the hold for about 2 to 3 seconds.

This encourages climbers to look at their feet and to be conscious of their foot placements.

IMPROVER DRILL

Skill Level: Beginner

Group Size: 1-20

For a variation on this drill, try combining it with **Hover Feet** (page 71). It also works well in the same session as **Sticky Eyes** (page 87).

HOVER HANDS

This exercise is good for climbers who are practising their flagging, and also works well as a warm-up activity.

Ask the climbers to choose a route to climb. Every time they wish to move a hand, they have to hover their hand about an inch away from the hold for about 3 to 5 seconds.

If the climber is in a bad position, with a chance of barn-dooring, they will lose energy, struggle and potentially fall off. Therefore, this exercise forces them to consider their body positioning and the need for flagging.

IMPROVER DRILL

Skill Level: Beginner

Group Size: 1-6

NOTE! – Be sure to seek permission from the centre first, as this drill often contradicts a centre's rules forbidding jumping off.

MAT TRUST

This exercise is useful for building confidence when climbing, and for learning how to fall correctly.

Explain that mats are there to help prevent injury. When falling off, it is important that we land feet first and bend our knees immediately to take the impact. Landing straight-legged increases the chance of injury.

Ask the climbers to climb up to head height and, after a countdown, to jump off. Remind them to focus on bending their knees.

Next, have the climbers climb up a foot higher and repeat the process. Keep increasing the height until they don't feel comfortable anymore. Always encourage, but never force them to do it!

Warm-Ups
Coordination
Techniques
Improver Drills
Group Management
Games
Team Building
Coaching
Resources
Recommended Drills

IMPROVER DRILL

Skill Level: Beginner

Group Size: 3-10

NINJA FEET

This drill is perfect for encouraging climbers to use quiet feet and to focus on their foot placements.

Ask the climbers to sit down in a line, about three metres from the wall, with their backs towards the wall. Choose a climber to get onto the wall, starting in the middle.

When you say 'Go!', the climber traverses for 30 to 45 seconds in either direction. After 30 to 45 seconds, shout 'Freeze!' and the climber stays where they are. Meanwhile, everyone else is sitting in the line with their backs to the wall, listening for the climber. Without looking, the climbers sitting down must guess where the climber is, purely by sound.

Make sure each climber starts in the same spot, and that they don't just stay still!

IMPROVER DRILL

Skill Level: Beginner

Group Size: 2-12

NINJA FEET 2

This drill is great for encouraging climbers to use quiet feet, and to focus on their foot placements.

Attach little bells to the shoes of the climbers, and ask them to climb an easy route of their choice. Tell them that they have to be as quiet as possible, and to avoid making any sound.

This drill forces the climber to make every foot placement slowly and concentrate entirely on their feet.

It works best in groups of two or three where the two climbers watching are the judges. You can add a points system, in which the climber loses a point every time they make a loud sound.

IMPROVER DRILL

Skill Level: Beginner

Group Size: 1-20

For a variation, try combining this with the **No Matching Drill** (page 73) or the **No Foot Adjustments Drill** (page 84).

9. NO FOOT SWAPPING

This exercise is good for climbers who are practising their route reading skills and foot placements.

This one is quite self-explanatory really; have the climbers climb multiple routes of mixed grades, during which they are not allowed to foot swap.

This encourages climbers to focus and think ahead about which foot to place where.

IMPROVER DRILL

Skill Level: Beginner

Group Size: 1-20

For a variation, try combining it with the **No Foot Swapping Drill** (page 73).

10. NO MATCHING

This exercise is perfect for climbers who are practising their route reading skills.

If necessary, begin by explaining that matching is a term for using both hands or both feet on the same hold.

This is another self-explanatory exercise; have the climbers climb multiple routes of mixed grades, during which they are not allowed to match with their hands.

IMPROVER DRILL

Skill Level: Beginner

Group Size: 1-16

OCTOPUS FEET

This drill is suited to younger climbers who are still learning their range of movement in climbing.

Ask the climbers to find a low-level jug with lots of holds surrounding it. See how many holds they can touch with their left foot, without releasing their hands from the jug.

Encourage them to reach in all different directions, including above their heads. Afterwards, ask the climbers to try the same exercise using their other foot.

This exercise works well in pairs too, with the second climber counting each foot tap and suggesting which holds to touch.

IMPROVER DRILL

Skill Level: Beginner

Group Size: 1-16

OCTOPUS HANDS

This drill is suited to younger climbers, who are still learning their range of movement in climbing.

Ask the climbers to find a low-level jug with lots of holds surrounding it. See how many holds they can touch with their left hand, without releasing their right hand from the jug.

Encourage them to go in all different directions, including below their feet. Afterwards, have the climbers try using their other hand.

This exercise works well in pairs too, with the second climber counting each hand tap and suggesting which holds to touch.

IMPROVER DRILL

Skill Level: Beginner

Group Size: 1-15

For a variation, try combining this with the **Windmill Drill** (page 129).

POINT AND GO

A really useful drill when teaching *Shifting Weight* and *Windmills*.

Ask the climbers to climb some vertical or slabby routes just below their normal grade. The climbers need to point, with one arm, in the direction that their body is moving as it moves.

For example, if they have a high right foot rockover, their right arm is going to point right as they completely shift the weight onto their right foot. Once they have shifted their weight, they are going to point straight up as they push their weight upwards and stand up.

IMPROVER DRILL

Skill Level: Beginner

Group Size: 1-20

STICKERS SHIFTING

This exercise is perfect for climbers learning and practising shifting weight, and for practising rockovers.

Place a sticker on the climber's belly button, and on the big toe area of both shoes. The climbers have to keep the stickers on during their climbing session. Every time they want to move their right foot, they first have to line up the sticker on their belly button with the sticker on their left foot.

Repeat this process with every move of every climb and with both feet. If the climber is in a situation where they need both feet on the wall at the same time, then the belly button sticker should be halfway between both feet.

IMPROVER DRILL

Skill Level: Beginner

Group Size: 1-20

15. STOP! 1,2,3

Split the climbers up into groups of 2-4, depending on the group size. You can also do this with only one climber, with you being the buddy at the bottom watching and listening.

Explain to the group that you want them to focus on climbing quietly. One person is going to climb, and the rest of the group will listen for any noise from the climber.

If the listeners hear any noises from the climber on the wall, they shout: '*Stop!*' The climber must then freeze in the exact position they are in, and the listeners shout: '*One! Two! Three!*'

After '*Three*', the climber resumes climbing, and the rest of the group keep listening. If the climber makes a noise again, they shout: '*Stop! One! Two! Three!*' Repeat this process until the climber finishes the climb.

IMPROVER DRILL

Skill Level: Novice

Group Size: 2-12

16. BEANBAG CHALLENGE

This exercise is great for encouraging dynamic climbing, and is a good team bonding exercise.

Split the group into pairs, and give Climber 1 a beanbag to hold in their left hand. Climber 2 has to hold the same beanbag with their right hand. Assign the climbers a wall to climb (using any holds), but explain that they are not allowed to let go of the beanbag.

There are many possible variations on this exercise and it can be a fun competitive game. Try turning it into a race to encourage dynamic climbing. Alternatively, challenge the climbers to climb the same route or perhaps specific neighbouring routes whilst holding the beanbag.

IMPROVER DRILL

Skill Level: Novice

Group Size: 1-2

If the climbers are still fairly new to climbing, try this exercise wearing only one boxing glove.

BOXING GLOVES

This exercise is perfect for encouraging climbers to climb slowly and statically, really focusing on shifting their weight. It also improves footwork, as in this exercise the feet need to take the majority of the climber's weight.

Ask the climber to choose a route below their normal grade. They should climb the route as they normally would; however, they have to wear boxing gloves! I find this a perfect drill after teaching *Shifting Weight* or *Pulling In with Feet*.

Boxing Gloves *– This exercise will force the climbers to climb slowly and statically, concentrating on their weight and footwork.*

IMPROVER DRILL

Skill Level: Novice

Group Size: 1-20

BUMPING

Personally, I like to have a drill for everything. This drill is ideal for teaching climbers to read routes, and to get out of the habit of climbing in a left-right-left-right sequence.

Explain to the climbers that they have 15 minutes to climb whichever routes they wish. However, every time they move a hand they have to move the same hand again a second time. So they will be climbing in a sequence of left hand and left hand again, then right hand and right hand again.

IMPROVER DRILL

Skill Level: Novice

Group Size: 1-15

CORK & BEANBAG ELIMINATION

This exercise is a fun drill, perfect for teaching route reading and foot placements.

Split the climbers into groups of 2-4. Ask each group to pick a route about two grades below their normal climbing level.

Have each climber climb the route once to gain a feel for it. Afterwards, ask each climber to put a cork or beanbag on a hold of their choice.

The climbers then have to climb the route without knocking off the cork or beanbag. Thereafter, you can either add more corks and beanbags, or simply move the items around.

You can include a points system to spice it up. Each time the climber knocks off a cork or beanbag, they gain a point. The climber with the fewest points wins.

IMPROVER DRILL

Skill Level: Novice

Group Size: 1-15

CORKS ON FOOTHOLDS

This exercise is great for encouraging precise foot placements and avoiding foot swaps.

Either choose a traverse wall or a vertical climb or slab. Place corks on footholds in varied positions. The climbers have to traverse or climb the route without knocking off any of the corks.

Include a points system to spice it up. Each time the climber knocks off a cork, they gain a point. The climber with the fewest points wins.

Warm-Ups | Coordination | Techniques | Improver Drills | Group Management | Games | Team Building | Coaching | Resources | Recommended Drills

IMPROVER DRILL

Skill Level: Novice

Group Size: 1-15

This is a great exercise to do after the **Speed Climbing Drill** (page 87), or the **Double Handed Drill** (page 78). It also works well in the same session as **Double Hand and Foot** (page 78).

DOUBLE FOOTED

This drill is ideal for improving a climber's dynamic climbing, deadpointing, coordination and confidence.

Ask the climbers to climb low-graded routes of their choice. However, every time they move a foot they have to move both feet at the same time, either to the same hold or to two different holds.

IMPROVER DRILL

Skill Level: Novice

Group Size: 1-15

DOUBLE HANDED

This drill is ideal for improving a climber's dynamic climbing, deadpointing, coordination and confidence.

Ask the climbers to climb low-graded routes of their choice. However, every time they move a hand they have to move both hands at the same time, either to the same hold or to two different holds.

IMPROVER DRILL

Skill Level: Novice

Group Size: 1-15

This makes a great follow-on to the **Double Footed Drill** and **Double Handed Drill** (above). It also works well in the same session as **Speed Climbing** (page 87) or **Tap and Go** (page 31).

DOUBLE HAND & FOOT

This drill is perfect for improving a climber's dynamic climbing, deadpointing, coordination and confidence.

Ask the climbers to climb low-graded routes of their choice. However, every time they move a hand, they have to move both hands at the same time. Also, every time they move a foot, they have to move both feet at the same time. In both cases this can either be to the same hold or to two different holds.

IMPROVER DRILL

Skill Level: Novice

Group Size: 2-16

24. ELIMINATION

Elimination is a fun game that improves a climber's route reading and footwork. It's also good for endurance and memory, and works best in groups of 2-5.

Each climber starts with three lives. As a group, they choose an easy climb with lots of holds. The first climber climbs the route, but chooses a hold to eliminate and completes the route without the use of this hold.

The second climber then has to climb the same route, without using the hold that has already been eliminated. Next, they must also choose a hold to eliminate and complete the route without the use of this hold.

If a climber uses a hold that is eliminated, or falls off, that climber loses a life. The game continues until all but one climber is out.

IMPROVER DRILL

Skill Level: Novice

Group Size: 1-20

25. FOOT TO HAND

This drill is great for practising footwork and slab climbing, and encourages climbers to focus on placing their feet onto holds.

Explain to the climbers that they have 15 minutes to climb any routes of their choice. However, every time they want to move a hand, they must first place a foot on the same hold as their hand.

For example, if they have their left hand on a hold, and are ready to grab a different hold with their left hand, they first need to place a foot on the hold that their left hand is currently on. Only then are they able to release their left hand.

Repeat this process, and encourage the climbers to experiment with gripping holds differently in order to make room for the incoming foot.

IMPROVER DRILL

Skill Level: Novice

Group Size: 1-10

FOOTWORK TAPE

This drill is perfect for climbers who are learning, or trying to improve their footwork. It also encourages climbers to use different parts of their shoes.

Before the session, find a wall around 8 to 10 metres long with a lot of different footholds. Next, place a thin strip of tape next to the precise part of each foothold that you would like them to use. Choose footholds in a variety of shapes and sizes.

Begin the session by placing 3 strips of tape on the climbers' shoes in such a way that they are easy for the climber to see:

1 - on their inside edge

2 - in the middle of the front of their shoe

3 - on their outside edge

The climbers must then traverse the wall using only the taped footholds. More specifically, they must only use the part of the hold where the tape is, each time lining up a piece of tape on their foot with a piece of tape on the hold.

This will force them to concentrate on their footwork by making them carefully stand front on, on their inside edge, or on their outside edge.

IMPROVER DRILL

Skill Level: Novice

Group Size: 1-12

FOOTWORK TEST

This exercise is perfect for teaching footwork, and is also a great way of analysing a climber's current footwork.

Before the session, find a 6 to 8 metre wall with lots of small footholds in a row. Grab some chalkboard chalk (I find blue chalk works best) and put some on each foothold.

When the session starts, explain to the group that they need to traverse the wall, using only the row of footholds that you have chosen. Don't tell them anything about the chalk, just ask them to traverse the wall.

Once the climbers have finished, ask them to sit down and look at the soles of their shoes. They will notice that the chalk will show up on their shoes where they have used their feet the most.

Obviously, if the chalk is in the middle of the shoe, you can explain to the climbers that they should be standing on the edges of their shoes, or on their toes.

For more experienced climbers, it will tell you which edges they use a lot and you can normally work out why. For example, if they are traversing right and their left foot has a lot of chalk on the outside edge, it normally indicates they are choosing to use the hop foot-swap more frequently than other, safer foot swaps.

IMPROVER DRILL

Skill Level: Novice

Group Size: 1-20

This exercise is best combined with the **Stickers Shifting Drill** (page 74). It also works well when combined with **Hover Hands** (page 71).

FLAGGING LINE

This exercise is ideal for climbers who are practising their flagging.

Put stickers on the climber's middle finger, where their belly button is, and on their shoe where their big toe is. Ask the climber to choose a route to climb. Every time the climber moves a hand, they have to flag a foot, and draw a direct line from the sticker on their finger through to their belly button and onto their toe.

IMPROVER DRILL

Skill Level: Novice

Group Size: 1-20

FLAG HAPPY

This exercise is perfect for climbers who are practising their flagging. It also works well as a warm-up activity.

Choose a route or a circuit, around 2 to 3 grades below the climber's normal level. Ask the climber to climb the route, specifically concentrating on each flag. Every time the climber wishes to move a hand, they are only allowed one foot on the wall. Quite often, they will have two feet on the wall, and will have to decide which leg to drop or flag with.

Ask them to consider which flag would be most appropriate for each move. If the climber is advanced, encourage them to incorporate inside flags and back flags.

IMPROVER DRILL

Skill Level: Novice

Group Size: 1-20

HEEL TO HAND

This drill is great for practising heel hooks, and is a variation of the *Foot to Hand* drill (page 173).

Explain to the climbers that they have 15 minutes to climb any routes of their choice. However, every time they want to move a hand, they must first place a heel hook onto the same hold as their hand.

For example, if they have their left hand on a hold, and want to grab a different hold with the left hand, they first have to place a heel hook on the hold that their left hand is currently on. Only then are they allowed to release their left hand.

Repeat this process, and encourage the climbers to experiment with holding holds differently in order to make room for the incoming heel. Sometimes I ban climbers from placing their heels on the top of holds, forcing them to heel hook the side.

__Heel to Hand__ – A simple exercise that encourages climbers to think about how they are using holds.

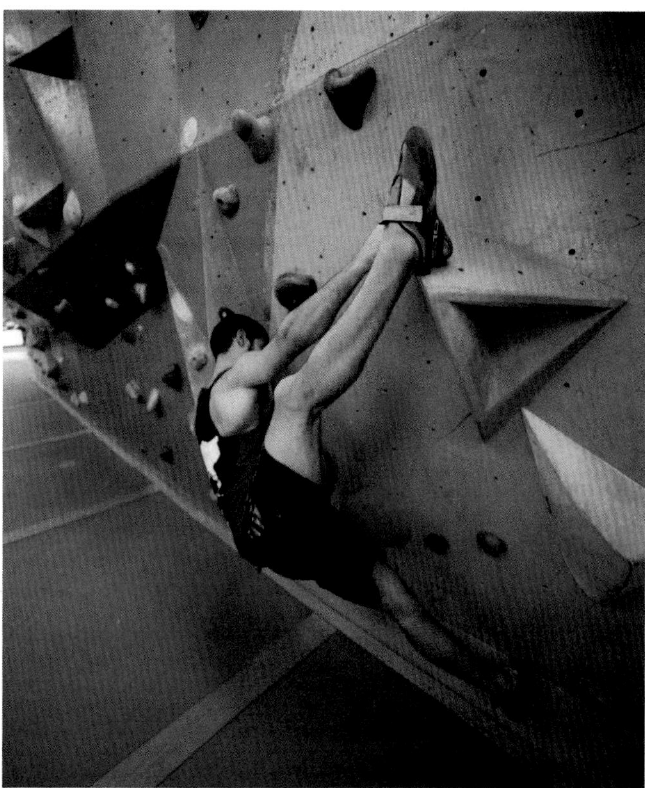

IMPROVER DRILL

Skill Level: Novice

Group Size: 1-20

MATCH EVERY HOLD

This exercise is perfect for improving a climber's matching ability.

If necessary, begin by explaining that matching is a term for using both hands or both feet on the same hold.

Pick a climb of a medium grade for your climbers. While they are climbing it they must match on every handhold they use. If possible, have them match on every handhold on the climb down too.

Match Every Hold – *A good way to practise matching, and a useful exercise in thinking about the way we move and use holds.*

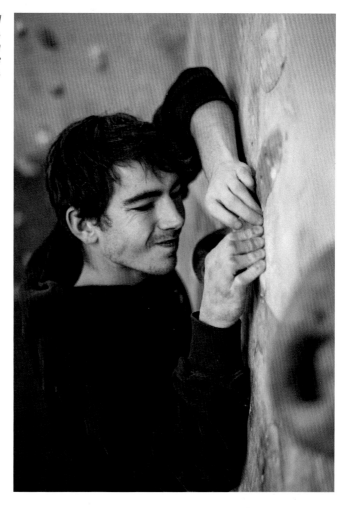

IMPROVER DRILL

Skill Level: Novice

Group Size: 1-20

NO FOOT ADJUSTMENTS

This exercise is perfect for climbers who are practising their footwork, and eliminates the bad habit of constantly adjusting a foot on a hold, normally on bad footholds.

Have the climbers continue their climbing session. However, whilst they climb, they are not allowed to pivot or adjust their foot on a hold. For example, if they place their foot on a hold with their outside edge, they have to remain on their outside edge until they move their foot onto their next foothold.

This encourages thoughtful foot placements on the wall. It is also great for route reading, as it makes you plan a move or two ahead.

IMPROVER DRILL

Skill Level: Novice

Group Size: 1-20

NO HANDS!

This exercise is perfect for helping people to discover ways of weighting their feet efficiently and finding resting points.

Allocate the climbers five minutes for this exercise. Within those five minutes, each climber must independently find as many positions as possible across the entire wall where they can completely let go with their hands.

An example of this is in a corner, whilst bridging. You have the option of awarding points for each different no-handed position a climber finds. With an experienced group you could make it more challenging by eliminating all forms of slabs.

IMPROVER DRILL

Skill Level: Novice

Group Size: 2-12

As a variation, try making the climbers climb the same route, or perhaps neighbouring routes.

ROPE CHALLENGE

This exercise is great for encouraging static climbing and route reading, and is also good for team bonding.

It is very similar to the *Beanbag Challenge* (page 75) and works well when combined within the same session.

Split the group into pairs, and ask each pair to join themselves together with a two foot rope, tucking the rope into the waistband of their shorts or trousers. Give the climbers a wall to climb (using any holds), but explain that they are not allowed to let their chain come undone.

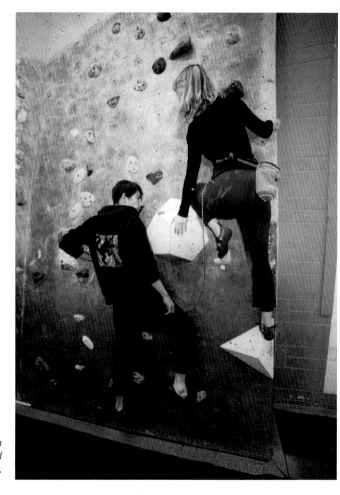

***Rope Challenge** – A fun game that's also a good team-building exercise.*

IMPROVER DRILL

Skill Level: Novice

Group Size: 1-12

Ask more advanced climbers to climb back down the route while still holding the tennis balls.

ROUNDED HANDS

This exercise is perfect for teaching climbers to shift their weight and practise their balance.

This drill can only be done on a very easy slab route with the option to rainbow climb (use any coloured holds). Ask the climbers to climb the slab while holding tennis balls in their hands. They are not allowed to grab any holds or let go of the tennis balls. They are only allowed to push the tennis balls against the flat wall, until they reach the top.

IMPROVER DRILL

Skill Level: Novice

Group Size: 1-20

A harder variation is **Smear, Smear, Step** (page 86), which works well after this drill.

SMEAR A FOOT

This exercise is good for climbers learning or honing their smearing skills.

Get the climbers to climb a route of their choice. They have to climb the route twice. The first time, they are only allowed to smear with their left foot, with their right foot being used as normal.

The second time, they are only allowed to smear with their right foot, with their left foot being used as normal.

IMPROVER DRILL

Skill Level: Novice

Group Size: 1-20

As a variation, ask the climbers to perform this exercise whilst climbing back down the route as well.

SMEAR, SMEAR, STEP

This is another exercise for climbers learning or honing their smearing skills.

Ask the climbers to climb some routes graded below their normal ability. Every time they want to move a foot, they need to do at least two smears first.

For example, if they want to move their left foot onto a different hold, they first have to smear with their left foot, smear with their right foot, and then place their left foot onto the hold. They repeat this process every time they wish to move a foot.

IMPROVER DRILL

Skill Level: Novice

Group Size: 1-15

Double Handed (page 78) is a great drill to do after the **Speed Climbing** exercise. Advanced climbers might like to try combining them.

SPEED CLIMBING

***Speed Climbing* is an amazing drill for improving a climber's dynamic climbing, deadpointing, coordination and confidence. It is also super fun!**

Choose a route graded below the climber's normal ability. Explain to the climber that they have to climb it as quickly as possible, and that you are going to time them. This exercise works best if you set them realistic goals. Get them to try the same climb 3 or 4 times before moving on.

Alternatively, you can set a 2 minute timer and challenge each climber to climb as many routes as possible within the time limit.

IMPROVER DRILL

Skill Level: Novice

Group Size: 1-20

SPRINGY CLIMBING

This drill is a great way to encourage climbers to get more dynamic in their climbing.

Ask the climbers to climb a variety of routes at their current grade for 10 to 15 minutes. Ask them to focus on doing each move in one dynamic motion. When they are ready to stand up and reach the hold, they have to begin from a fully bent-leg position with their arms straight. From that position, they stand up in one dynamic motion towards their handhold.

Repeat this process for the duration of the drill.

IMPROVER DRILL

Skill Level: Novice

Group Size: 1-15

STICKY EYES

This is a really good drill for improving a climber's footwork and foot placements.

Explain that a lot of climbers develop a bad habit of looking away from their feet as they place them onto a hold. Obviously, this encourages bad foot placements.

Ask the climbers to climb routes at their normal grades. However, every time they want to move a foot, they have to stare at the foothold they wish to use. They need to look at the hold before, during and slightly after they place their foot onto the hold. Once their foot is on the hold, they are allowed to look away.

Repeat this process throughout the entire climb, and attempt multiple routes to develop this skill.

Warm-Ups
Coordination
Techniques
Improver Drills
Group Management
Games
Team Building
Coaching
Resources
Recommended Drills

IMPROVER DRILL

Skill Level: Novice

Group Size: 1-15

41 TRAVERSE CHALLENGES

This drill is also great when used as a warm-up, and to practise techniques covered on previous sessions.

Pick a starting point and finishing point on a wall, and have the climbers traverse from the starting point to the finishing point. Once they have finished, have them start at the beginning again. In between each turn, ask them to focus on a specific technique.

For example, on their first traverse, ask them to focus on foot-swaps. If they are experienced climbers, you can ask them to focus on a specific foot swap, e.g. The Table Cloth.

Next, ask them to focus on something else such as 'straight arms'. Repeat this process and continue to add a new technique on every rotation.

IMPROVER DRILL

Skill Level: Novice

Group Size: 1-15

42 WEIGHTED FEET MEANS REST!

This drill is perfect for helping people to discover ways of weighting their feet efficiently and finding resting points. It works best on slightly slabby climbs.

Ask the climber to choose a route around their best grade or slightly below. Inform the climber that every three to four moves they must adjust their position, find their balance, and completely let go with their hands for 3 seconds before continuing.

Alternatively, on harder routes, ask the climbers to look for one resting position during the climb.

IMPROVER DRILL

Skill Level: Intermediate

Group Size: 2-10

As a variation, ask the climbers to climb the same route four times in a row.

4x4 CLIMBING

This exercise is a great way of increasing a climber's endurance, power endurance, route reading and skills in different styles of climbing.

Split the group into teams of two, paired with climbers of a similar ability. Pick four routes 2 to 3 grades below their normal flash ability. For example, if they can flash 6b+, they should climb 6a/6a+.

Each four routes make up one set. Make sure that each set includes a variety of climbing styles, for example: vertical / overhang / slab / vertical.

Climber 1 climbs first, with Climber 2 picking the routes for him to climb. As soon as Climber 1 has finished a climb and reached the floor, he gets straight onto the next climb, and keeps going until he has finished the set of four.

Once Climber 1 has finished, he then picks the routes for Climber 2, and the process starts again. Aim to do two to three sets per climber.

IMPROVER DRILL

Skill Level: Intermediate

Group Size: 1-16

ADD A MOVE

This is a fun exercise, especially when the climbers are of a similar grade. *Add a Move* works best in groups of 2-5. It is great for improving footwork, endurance and memory.

Each climber starts with three lives. The first climber chooses a starting handhold, gets onto the wall, and then makes a move to another handhold of their choice. The second climber then does the same two moves, and then adds a new handhold afterwards. If a climber falls off before making their next move, they lose a life. This process continues until there is only one climber left in the game.

During the game, the climbers are allowed to use any footholds as they climb, but must stick to the designated handholds. Their hands also have to remain sequential; if Climber 1 moves their left hand first, everyone must follow in the same order, moving their left hand first too.

IMPROVER DRILL

Skill Level: Intermediate

Group Size: 1-15

Variations on this exercise are to allow an additional colour for one foot only, or to allow a certain number of additional holds for the whole climb.

ADDITIONAL COLOURS

This drill is perfect for improving a climber's grip strength and footwork ability. It is also a good drill for regular climbers who have exhausted a centre and are awaiting a new set.

Explain to the climbers that they are going to climb routes above their grade, or potentially the hardest grade in the centre.

Whilst climbing they have to stick to the normal colour with their hands, but they are allowed to use any colour for their feet.

IMPROVER DRILL

Skill Level: Intermediate

Group Size: 1-20

This drill works well when combined with **Hover 90°** (page 116).

ADJUSTING HOLDS

This is a great drill for improving a climber's route reading ability and static climbing.

Allow the climbers to climb any routes they wish for 15 minutes. However, every time they grab a handhold, they then need to use the hold differently. For example, if they grab a sloper with their fingers pointing left, they must adjust their grip and hold it any other possible way (e.g. with their fingers pointing right). Once they have adjusted their grip, they are allowed to make their next move.

IMPROVER DRILL

Skill Level: Intermediate

Group Size: 1-10

As a variation, challenge the climbers to do the traverse using as few holds as possible.

BALANCE TRAVERSE

This drill is perfect for improving a climber's footwork, balance, slab climbing and static climbing ability.

This drill only works on a wall that is slabby enough for you to lean forward and let go with your hands. Pick a starting hold and a finish hold. Explain to the climbers that they need to traverse from the starting hold to the finishing hold without using their hands.

IMPROVER DRILL

Skill Level: Intermediate

Group Size: 1-15

48. BLINDFOLDED ROUTE READING

This exercise is perfect for encouraging climbers to read routes, and not just launch straight into the climb before they have properly visualised the moves.

Choose a problem for each climber that is significantly below their normal level; for example, if the climber usually boulders at V4 or Font 6b, then pick something about V2 or Font 5.

Explain to the climbers that they must climb the problem without touching any other coloured holds – each time they do so they will lose one point. Also mention that before they begin, they will be given one minute to study the route and memorise exactly where they are going.

The climbers will probably look puzzled and immediately say 'OK – I'm ready now.'

As they are about to get onto the wall, ask them to stop and put on a blindfold. They will almost certainly rethink and ask for another minute.

Not knowing that they would be blindfolded highlights to the climber the fact that when looking at the route, they have not actually been reading the moves – hence the need for a second look.

IMPROVER DRILL

Skill Level: Intermediate

Group Size: 2-20

49. BLINDFOLD TAG

Choose a strip of wall around 6 to 8 metres long and select a starting hold and a finishing hold. Place red and green rugby tags across the wall on different holds.

Explain to the climbers that they will start on the first hold, and traverse across the wall to the finishing hold. If they touch or drop a red tag, they will lose a point. If they grab a green tag, they gain a point.

Give them as much time as they want to look at their route, but explain to them that they will be blindfolded as soon as they are ready to climb.

IMPROVER DRILL

Skill Level: Intermediate

Group Size: 1-6

50. CHUCK CLIMBING

This exercise is amazing for improving a climber's grip strength, endurance, footwork and balance.

Ask the climbers to pick a climb about 5 to 6 grades below their climbing grade. Alternatively, have them rainbow climb (use any colours). Inform the climbers that they must hold onto the wooden chucks with their hands, and they are not allowed to hold anything else.

The objective is to simply climb the wall, hooking the wooden chucks onto the holds. This drill encourages body positioning and flagging, as the climbers will need to ensure they are in balance when trying to move.

IMPROVER DRILL

Skill Level: Intermediate

Group Size: 1-15

51. CIRCLE CLIMBING

This exercise is perfect for putting climbers into unusual climbing positions.

Use tape to mark out a circle on the wall, with a diameter of approximately 2 feet. Ask the climbers to climb around the circled area three times.

First attempt – They are allowed to have their feet inside the circled area, but have to avoid using their hands inside the circle.

Second attempt – They are allowed their hands inside the circled area, but have to avoid using their feet inside the circle.

Third attempt – They are not allowed any part of their body inside the circled area and have to avoid the circle altogether.

CLOCKWORK

IMPROVER DRILL

Skill Level: Intermediate

Group Size: 1-20

This drill is ideal for encouraging climbers to experiment with different hand movements, and is useful for teaching climbers that you don't always need to climb upwards to progress.

The climbers need to climb routes way below their normal grade. Explain that each hand movement must be in a trio sequence. Every time they move their left hand up, they then need to move their right hand up and then their left hand down. Next, they bring their feet up the wall, before repeating the process. So they move their right hand up, followed by their left hand up, and then bring their right hand back down.

DOWN CLIMB

IMPROVER DRILL

Skill Level: Intermediate

Group Size: 1-15

This exercise is useful for helping climbers to learn how to get out of a situation where they have gone the wrong way, but are still striving for that all-important flash. This drill is also good for encouraging accurate foot placements.

Ask the climbers to pick a climb at their crux grade. Inform the climbers that they need to rainbow (use holds of any colour) to get to the top of their chosen climb. Once they have reached the last hold, they need to match on the hold and then get their feet onto the appropriate colour before climbing down the chosen coloured route.

DYNO DRILL

IMPROVER DRILL

Skill Level: Intermediate

Group Size: 1-15

A great drill for practising dynos and dynamic climbing. It is also useful for improving a climber's coordination.

Ask the climbers to go around the centre and try each climb in the lowest-graded circuit, for example all of the greys (V0). Explain to the climbers that on each problem they must dyno from their starting holds, aiming for the furthest hold they think they can reach.

They have two attempts. On their first attempt, they need to dyno as far as they can with only one hand. On their second attempt, they need to dyno as far as they can double-handed.

IMPROVER DRILL

Skill Level: Intermediate

Group Size: 1-15

55. DYNO LADDER

This exercise is great for improving a climber's ability to dyno.

Ask the climbers to try a climb of the lowest-graded circuit (V0 / Font 3). They should start on the starting handholds, and are allowed to use any of the footholds of that route.

Explain that they need to dyno from their starting holds to the next handhold. Next, they need to dyno from the starting holds to the next hold after that one, eliminating the previous hold.

Repeat until they have hit their limit hold, and ask them to repeat that biggest dyno three times. Obviously, you can skip the first few holds when doing this drill.

IMPROVER DRILL

Skill Level: Intermediate

Group Size: 1-10

56. DYNO TAPED

An excellent drill for improving a climber's dyno ability.

A lot of people work harder once they have a target or goal to beat. Simply ask the climber to dyno as high as they can from a couple of jugs. Place a piece of tape on the wall to mark their high point.

Then simply ask them to repeat the dyno and aim to beat their taped marker. When they beat their marker, make a new marker and have that as the next goal to beat. Repeat for 5 minutes, and then vary the holds and direction of the dyno.

IMPROVER DRILL

Skill Level: Intermediate

Group Size: 1-15

57. DYNO TIME

This exercise is great for improving a climber's ability to dyno. It is best done before teaching climbers how to dyno.

Before the session starts, find 3 or 4 examples of dynos. Ask the climbers to attempt each dyno once, and mark or remember how close they got to the hold which they were aiming for on each dyno. This exercise works best with dynos that are too far, as you don't want them to reach the target hold first go.

Then, call the group together and teach them the techniques for dynos (page 46). Once they are all comfortable with the techniques, ask them to attempt each dyno again, and see if they can get higher than their previous marks.

IMPROVER DRILL

Skill Level: Intermediate

Group Size: 1-15

FEET PULLING

This is a good drill to do after teaching climbers *Pulling in With Feet* (page 101).

Give the climbers 10 minutes to climb routes graded one or two grades below their normal level. Remind the group that they need to focus on pulling in with their feet, and not their arms.

Explain that every time they want to move their right hand, they first need to let go with their right hand, and then use their right foot to pull themselves upwards and towards the hold.

Repeat this process and encourage climbers to avoid simply flagging into every move to make it easy – instead ask them to focus on pulling in with their feet.

IMPROVER DRILL

Skill Level: Intermediate

Group Size: 2-12

FOOTWORK COMPETITION

This is a perfect drill for improving footwork. It works best with a group of similar abilities.

Split the group into two teams and give each team some tape. Explain to the group that both teams will have an area and that they are in direct competition with each other.

The teams have 10 minutes to set a traverse for each other between a given starting handhold and finishing handhold.

Explain that they need to place tape onto some footholds leaving only parts of the footholds available for the other team to use. The climbers are only allowed to use the footholds with tape on them.

After 10 minutes, a climber from Team 1 must demo the route they have set. If the climber falls off during the demo, the other team gains a point. The climber then gets another go at demonstrating the route, handing a point to Team 2 each time they fall off.

Once the demo is complete, every member of Team 2 must attempt the traverse. If a climber flashes the problem, their team gains a point. If a climber falls off, the other team gains a point.

Keep track of scores, and once everyone from Team 2 has had their attempt at the traverse, move onto Team 2's traverse, starting with their demo.

Warm-Ups
Coordination
Techniques
Improver Drills
Group Management
Games
Team Building
Coaching
Resources
Recommended Drills

IMPROVER DRILL

● ● ●

Skill Level: Intermediate

Group Size: 1-12

As a variation, ask them to try and sit in the rocked-over position and let go with their hands. This will only work if they are fully rocked over and perfectly in balance.

HEEL HOOK ROCKOVERS

This exercise is good for climbers who are practising their heel hooks and rockovers.

Set the climbers a rockover with a high foot, above their waist height. Ask the climbers to try the rockover twice: first with a high toe, and secondly with a high heel. Ask them which they feel is easier and why. If the rockover is set correctly, they will normally say the heel hook.

During the rockover, remind them to focus on shifting their weight over their foot before making progress up the wall.

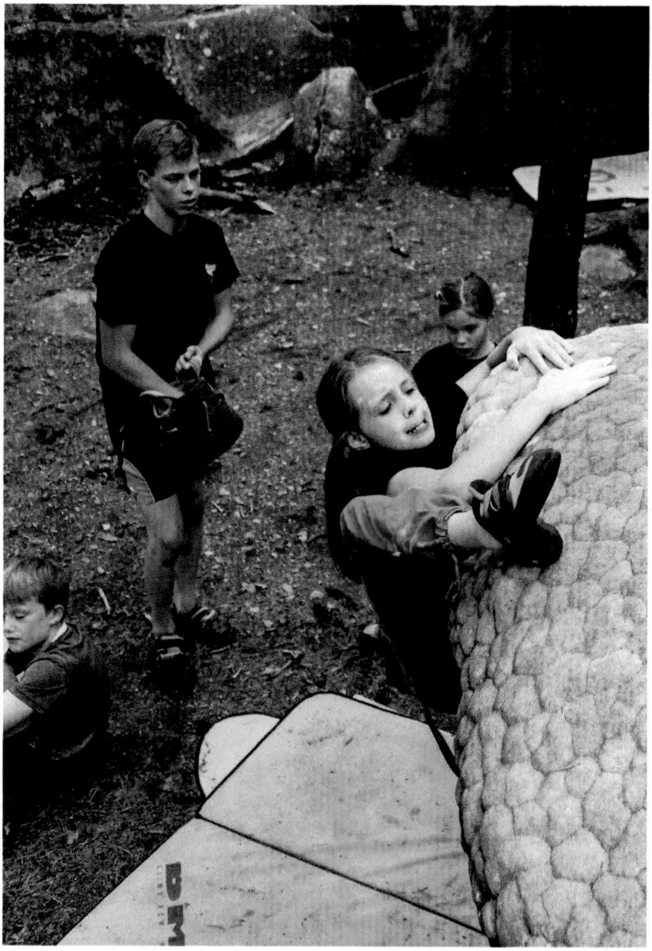

Heel Hook Rockovers – A technique that is common in outdoor bouldering, but requires practice.

IMPROVER DRILL

Skill Level: Intermediate

Group Size: 1-6

HEEL STARTS

This drill is great for climbers learning how to heel hook, and how to effectively engage the heel when climbing.

Simply choose two different handholds for the climber to hold on to, with their feet still on the floor. Then point to another hold – the climber must place their heel onto this hold, engage the heel, and release their other foot from the floor.

It also works well if you pick a hold to rock up to once the heel is weighted. Continue this routine on varied holds. Vary the size and quality of both the handholds and footholds.

IMPROVER DRILL

Skill Level: Intermediate

Group Size: 1-20

This drill is perfect when combined with **Hover 90°** (page 116), and works well before the **Adjusting Holds** drill (page 90).

LOCK AND TEST

This exercise is perfect when teaching climbers to climb more statically and to experiment with different holds. It is a great drill for improving a climber's strength and lock ability.

Explain to the climbers that they may climb any routes of their choice. However, every time they want to move a hand, they have to initially lock their arm at either 90 degrees or in full lock, and feel the hold they are about to grab before using it. They should repeat this throughout their climbs.

IMPROVER DRILL

Skill Level: Intermediate

Group Size: 1-15

MILEAGE

Climbing is the best way to improve at climbing.

Split the group up into pairs or groups of three. Ask the groups to pick a circuit (or colour) and attempt to climb each route within that circuit.

For example, they must go around the entire climbing centre and complete every blue route in the building.

Explain that they have up to three attempts each per problem, after which they should move on to the next problem.

IMPROVER DRILL

Skill Level: Intermediate

Group Size: 1-16

MULTI-AREA STYLES

This exercise is perfect for encouraging climbers to try different styles of climbing and discover where their weaknesses are.

This drill can be done either in groups of 3 or 4 climbers or with an individual. Each group is assigned to one of the following areas:

Roof / Slab / Overhang / Vertical

Each group has twenty minutes in their area. They have to attempt three different climbs at their crux grade, and they have three attempts each. Afterwards, they have a game of *Add a Move* (page 89), still in their designated area.

When 20 minutes is up, call the group in, and ask for feedback regarding their weaknesses – for example 'dynamic moves on an overhang'. Then simply rotate the group around the areas and repeat the process.

IMPROVER DRILL

Skill Level: Intermediate

Group Size: 1-15

MULTI-STYLES

This exercise is perfect for encouraging climbers to try problems both statically and dynamically.

If necessary, begin by explaining the difference between dynamic climbing and static climbing.

Dynamic Climbing – Normally involves momentum to help make progress on the wall.

Static Climbing – Normally involves slower movement, in a more balanced, steady fashion.

Pick a climb of a medium grade for your climbers. Each climber should try the route three times. First, ask them to climb it as dynamically as possible. Second, ask them to climb it as statically as possible. Finally, ask them to try to combine both static and dynamic climbing to get the best possible results.

IMPROVER DRILL

Skill Level: Intermediate

Group Size: 1-15

PALM EVERY MOVE

Allocate a set time (for example, 10 minutes) for climbers to carry out this drill. Each climber can climb any route they wish within the time.

Every time the climber wants to move a foot, they must palm off the wall first. Repeat this process for every foot move they make.

It can be more effective to not inform them which hand they should palm with for each movement, instead letting them discover this for themselves. However, do be ready to point it out if required: for example, if they are moving their right foot, they need to palm with their right hand.

This drill is also perfect for helping climbers naturally understand when palming would be useful.

IMPROVER DRILL

Skill Level: Intermediate

Group Size: 1-10

PIVOTING A FOOT

This drill is great for practising footwork and foot-eye coordination.

Ask the climbers to get onto the wall with reasonable handholds, whilst smearing directly beneath their handholds.

Then ask the climbers to place their left foot on a hold out left and stand up onto the hold, whilst pivoting from an inside edge to an outside edge.

Next ask the climbers to place a foot on a hold out right, and stand up and pivot onto their right foot, with their left foot leaving its current hold.

Repeat this process, and vary the height and size of the footholds.

IMPROVER DRILL

Skill Level: Intermediate

Group Size: 1-15

68. POINTY ADD ON

***Pointy Add On* is a fun drill, especially when the climbers are of a similar grade. It works best in groups of 2-5 and is great for training endurance and footwork.**

The exercise is a combination of *Pointy Stick* and *Add a Move*.

Each climber starts with three lives. The first climber gets onto the wall in a starting position of their choice. The second climber then points to a hold and says 'Left hand' or 'Right hand'. The climber has to obey the command, but can use any footholds to get there.

They then jump off, and the second climber has to repeat the moves, with the third climber pointing to the hold that they have to go to next.

During the game, the climbers are allowed to use any footholds as they climb, but must stick to the designated handholds. Their hands also have to remain sequential, so if Climber 1 moves their left hand first, everyone else must do the same and follow in the same order. The climber is allowed to go in any direction they wish, provided they stick to the correct handholds.

IMPROVER DRILL

Skill Level: Intermediate

Group Size: 1-16

POINTY STICK

This exercise is great for training endurance and footwork.

Split the climbers into pairs. One person will be climbing and the other holding a long stick or brush with which to point.

The first climber gets onto the wall in a starting position of their choice. The second climber then points to a hold and says 'Left hand' or 'Right hand'. The climber has to obey the command, but can use any footholds to get there. The person with the stick then points to another hold, and repeats this process until the climber falls off.

Keep an eye out to ensure that the person with the stick doesn't add an impossible move. Try to get the climber to make as many moves as possible.

IMPROVER DRILL

Skill Level: Intermediate

Group Size: 1-12

PROBLEM MAKING

This exercise is perfect for encouraging and testing climbers on their knowledge of different climbing techniques. It can be done as individuals or in a group or team.

Write down some different climbing techniques on small pieces of paper and put them into a chalk bag. Ask each climber to pick 3 or 4 pieces of paper from the bag at random.

The climbers then need to create a boulder problem which includes all of the movements or techniques they picked out.

If there is more than one group, you can have each group try each other's boulder problems, and see if they climb them as planned.

IMPROVER DRILL

Skill Level: Intermediate

Group Size: 1-12

A cool variation is to have both feet on the wall and focus on pulling your hips in towards the wall without bending your arms.

PULLING WITH FEET

This drill is a perfect drill to do after teaching climbers *Pulling in with Feet* (page 60).

Ask the climbers to get onto a wall with a high left foot, and then rock over onto their foot, aiming to have their belly button over their foot. However, ask them to try to keep their arms straight the whole time. This means they have to really focus on pulling in with their left foot.

Next, ask them to smear both feet underneath their handholds and repeat the same motion onto another foothold on their right side. Repeat this process 3 to 4 times before moving to a different wall.

IMPROVER DRILL

Skill Level: Intermediate

Group Size: 1-12

RESTRICTED ARMS

This exercise is excellent for teaching shifting weight.

Ask the climbers to climb a low-grade route on a slab. Explain to the climber that they must climb the route but they are not allowed to bring their hands up above their head. This stops them from being able to pull themselves up with their arms.

Now repeat the same climb, but this time they are not allowed to bring their hands above chest height. If possible, the next step is to repeat the same climb without bringing their hands above their belly button. As they climb, they have to constantly palm down on the wall, pushing on holds, without being able to pull up with their arms.

IMPROVER DRILL

Skill Level: Intermediate

Group Size: 1-8

ROOF BATTLE

A fun game that is great for building strength, core, endurance and roof-climbing technique.

Split the group into pairs and ask everyone to sit down in front of the roof. Nominate a pair to go first. Both climbers choose a starting point anywhere on the roof.

When you say 'Go', the game has started and the last climber remaining on the wall is the winner. They are allowed to climb towards each other and tackle the other climber off the wall, within reason of course!

IMPROVER DRILL

Skill Level: Intermediate

Group Size: 1-6

ROOF HUG

This drill is a great core exercise, and is good for teaching climbers how to engage muscles.

Split the group into pairs. Ask Climber 1 to deadhang on some jugs on the roof, with Climber 2 standing next to them. Climber 1 then wraps their legs around the waist of Climber 2, who must then try to run away. Climber 1 has to try and keep hold of Climber 2 without letting go of their handholds.

IMPROVER DRILL

Skill Level: Intermediate

Group Size: 1-15

SET LADDER

Have a list of your climbing wall's grading order, from lowest to highest:

For example: Grey – Yellow – Orange – Purple – Blue – Blue & White – Red – Red & White - White

Pick an isolated wall or a new set, and explain to the climbers that they have to work their way up the grades. Everyone must start on the easiest colour (grey) and climb every single one of them. Once they have climbed all the greys, they can then try the next colour up (yellow).

They may do the routes of each colour in any order, but cannot move on to the next colour until every climb is completed. Once they hit their crux grade, encourage the climbers to share beta and help each other.

IMPROVER DRILL

Skill Level: Intermediate

Group Size: 1-4

SIT START DRILL

This drill is perfect for climbers practising their sit start abilities.

Ask the climber to sit on the mat next to a wall. Simply point to two starting handholds, and one or two starting footholds.

When the climber is in the starting position, point to another hold and say, 'Left hand' or, 'Right hand'. When the climber has made the move, ask them to sit back down and pick out some new holds.

Be sure to vary the types of wall, doing some sit starts on slabs, and some on vertical walls and overhangs. I find this drill works perfectly on a 40-degree board in private tuition sessions.

During this drill, you can help hone a climber's twisting, flagging and foot placement.

IMPROVER DRILL

Skill Level: Intermediate

Group Size: 1-6

SLAB OCTOPUS

A brilliant and much harder variation of *Octopus Feet* (page 73), this drill is perfect for practising awkward slab moves, foot positioning, shifting weight and for building leg strength.

Split the group into pairs and have the first climber climb a metre off the floor on a slabby wall. Ask them to find a large foothold for their left foot, then release their hands and right foot from the holds so they are standing only on their left foot. Explain that they are not allowed to use any of their other limbs for this drill.

Ask Climber 2 to point to a hold, which Climber 1 then needs to touch with their free foot (in this case, their right foot).

Repeat this process for 5 or 6 different holds, and then swap legs. Make sure that Climber 2 points to holds in all directions, including above and below.

Finally, swap roles and repeat the exercise with Climber 1 pointing out holds for Climber 2.

IMPROVER DRILL

Skill Level: Intermediate

Group Size: 1-20

This drill can be easily combined with **Rounded Hands** (page 86).

SMEAR TRUST

This exercise is perfect for climbers who are confident in their smearing, but are trying to hone their skills.

Start off with the climber traversing a slab, using anything for their hands but only smearing for their feet.

If that is too easy, repeat the exercise, but this time only allow the climber to use one hand.

Depending on the incline of the slab and the ability of the climber, repeat the exercise one more time, eliminating all handholds so that the climber is simply palming the flat wall.

IMPROVER DRILL

Skill Level: Intermediate

Group Size: 1-15

STAB AND GO

This drill is great for practising foot-eye coordination, and foot placements.

Have the climbers stand in front of a wall with lots of small footholds, then take 2 small steps back from the wall. From here they need to stab their left foot onto a hold and then stand up on the foothold towards a high handhold of their choice.

As soon as their foot lands on the foothold they are not allowed to readjust it. Repeat, swapping feet with every go, and varying the foothold size and height.

IMPROVER DRILL

Skill Level: Intermediate

Group Size: 1-15

STARTING POSITIONS

A great drill for climbers trying to improve their body positioning.

Ask the climbers to go around the hardest circuit in the centre (for example, the black circuit). Explain that they must pull onto every black climb in the circuit and hold the starting position for 3 seconds.

They don't need to be able to do a move, but should try to hold the starting position with both feet off the floor as if they have started the climb.

IMPROVER DRILL

Skill Level: Intermediate

Group Size: 1-15

81 TACKY SHOES

This exercise is perfect for climbers learning or honing their foot placement skills. It encourages climbers to place each foot slowly, and to concentrate on standing on their big toes.

Explain to the climbers that it is important to apply pressure to the foothold whenever possible. This is easiest to do by applying pressure / power through your big toe. With every foot placement that involves the inside edge or front-on placement, they should aim to stand on their big toe as much as possible. This also applies during foot swaps.

Attach a little sausage of sticky tack along the edge of the boots of each climber, covering the little toe and outside edge, all the way to the big toe. Ask each climber to climb five routes graded slightly below their normal crux ability. In between each climb, examine the sticky tack to see its shape.

IMPROVER DRILL

Skill Level: Intermediate

Group Size: 1-15

82 WRONG POSITIONS

This exercise is aimed at helping climbers figure out how to get unstuck when they accidentally end up in a bad position, such as wrong footed or facing the wrong way.

Choose an unstylish starting position on the wall. Then choose a finishing position that is more appropriate and orthodox.

Explain to the climbers that they can use any holds to get into the starting position, but they can only use the selected holds to turn themselves around and fix their body positioning. You can add a designated hand or foothold to help.

For example, choose a starting position on a slab with two footholds, but have the climbers wrong-footed so they are facing outwards. Then, have a left palm where, ideally, you would expect a right palm. The finish position is simply facing the wall with a right palm.

IMPROVER DRILL

Skill Level: Advanced

Group Size: 5-20

83. ANXIETY PREP

This drill is only for advanced climbers who are competing on a regular basis. I do this drill with my squad before a big competition to try to manage anxiety and nerves.

Explain to the group that the objective is for them to understand what makes them nervous and to see if they can determine some coping methods. They will have 30 to 40 minutes to complete the following tasks:

1) Audience – Ask them to find a climb at their hardest grade. After the time period is up, they will take turns to climb their route in front of the entire group, as well as any additional strangers who are floating around the wall.

2) Competition – During the time period, they must go over to the pull up bar and do as many pull ups as they can possibly do. Put up a score sheet for everyone's scores, on which they must record their result alongside those of their colleagues.

3) Video analysis – Ask them to find a climb at a hard grade, which they will need to climb super-efficiently and gracefully. Explain that once they have chosen and practised the climb, you or one of the other coaches will film it, and that you are going to send it off to the British team coaches for analysis (be sure to tell them at the end of the session that this isn't true).

Feel free to add more tasks too. A dyno competition is always good, with tape to mark their progress.

Before the session, give each climber a sheet on which to record their anxiety levels (an example is shown opposite). Just before they get onto the wall, they should fill in the sheet to record how their body feels, and how their mind feels.

At the end of the drill, call everyone in and explain that you are trying to help them realise what exactly makes them nervous. Encourage them to discuss as a team ways of dealing with nerves.

Anxiety Prep – Recording how we feel before an exercise helps us to look back and analyse what was making us feel nervous..

Anxiety Prep Exercises

1) **Audience**:

How does my mind feel? 1 2 3 4 5 6 7 8 9 10

How does my body feel? 1 2 3 4 5 6 7 8 9 10

2) **Competition**:

How does my mind feel? 1 2 3 4 5 6 7 8 9 10

How does my body feel? 1 2 3 4 5 6 7 8 9 10

3) **Video Analysis**:

How does my mind feel? 1 2 3 4 5 6 7 8 9 10

How does my body feel? 1 2 3 4 5 6 7 8 9 10

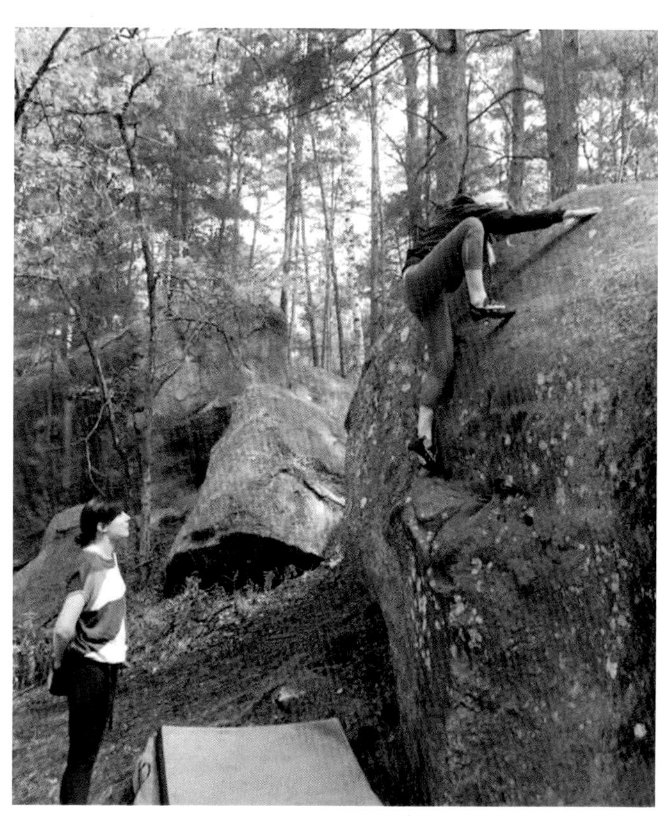

IMPROVER DRILL

Skill Level: Advanced

Group Size: 1-15

AVOID THE CUT

This exercise is perfect for improving a climber's core strength and overhang / roof climbing ability.

Pick a climb at or just below the climber's crux grade. The climber has to climb the route, but must avoid any form of a cut loose (cutting loose is where your feet come off the wall completely).

In the event of accidentally cutting loose, the climber has to climb down, have a rest and start again. Repeat on various climbs, being super-strict with the rules.

IMPROVER DRILL

Skill Level: Advanced

Group Size: 1-20

BAD BETA

This exercise is really useful for competitors, especially juniors, and is also a lot of fun.

During a competition, I noticed that a lot of random parents and inexperienced climbers were giving advice to our competition squad, who have a much greater understanding of technique themselves. However, as the squad were both nervous and extremely polite, they always listened to the bad advice.

Explain to the group that they get to climb routes of their choice for twenty minutes. During this time, walk around and offer them some subtle bad tips.

As time goes on, give them increasingly worse beta, eventually getting a little bit extreme:

'Have you tried getting a toe hook above your head?'

'Skip out the jug and go straight up for the terrible foothold. Trust me, I'm a coach.'

'Have you tried facing the other way, so your back is towards the wall?'

Call them in after twenty minutes and ask if they noticed anything different about their session. Guide them towards commenting on your bad advice and ask them if they should trust their own technique. Give some examples of previous competitions where / if you have noticed this.

***Bad Beta** – competition climbers may often get 'bad beta' from onlookers. Help them to trust their own abilities and be prepared for such occasions.*

IMPROVER DRILL

Skill Level: Advanced

Group Size: 1-4

CAUTION! – Be sure to have an experienced spotter for this drill.

86. BAT HANG CLIMBING

This fun drill is perfect for improving a climber's toe hooking and bat hang ability.

This exercise only works on an overhang with lots of big jugs. Pick a climb way below the climber's normal grade, or alternatively, let them use any holds. Have them start the climb in a bat hang position.

Explain that they have to climb the route but that they must lead with their feet, meaning they are only allowed to use toe hooks for their feet, and only on holds that are above their heads.

IMPROVER DRILL

Skill Level: Advanced

Group Size: 1-15

87. BREATHING CONTROL

Breathing provides our muscles with oxygen, which is something that they can't work without. Breathing properly will reduce the speed at which we get tired or pumped.

During the climbing session, ask the climbers to focus on their breathing. Before each climb, ask them to fill their body with oxygen by taking ten deep breaths. At the end of the climb, as soon as the climber reaches the floor, encourage them to take another ten deep breaths to speed up their recovery time.

Whilst climbing, ask them to pause every 2 or 3 moves and take 2 or 3 big breaths. Explain that, when possible, they should be resting with entirely straight arms so that their muscles are relaxed and receiving as much oxygen as possible.

IMPROVER DRILL

Skill Level: Advanced

Group Size: 1-16

88. CAMPUS ADD-ON

This drill is a harder version of *Add a Move* (page 89), which focuses on increasing a climber's campus ability.

Each climber starts with three lives. The first climber chooses a starting handhold, and then makes a move to a handhold of their choice. The second climber then does the same two moves, and adds a new handhold afterwards. If a climber falls off before making their next move, they lose a life. This process continues until there is only one person left in the game.

During the game, the climbers are not allowed to use their feet, and they have to stick to the designated handholds. Their hands also have to remain sequential, so if Climber 1 moves their left hand first, everyone else must do the same, moving their left hand first too.

IMPROVER DRILL

Skill Level: Advanced

Group Size: 1-30

COMPETITION

This exercise requires a bit of preparation, as you will need to create some scorecards and pick some routes before the session. It is perfect for competition preparation.

Fifteen to twenty routes normally works best for this drill. Include plenty of easy, confidence-building climbs, lots of medium-range climbs, and a couple of really hard climbs. Give the climbers a set time as a way of adding some pressure to the competition. Set up a scoring system in the following format:

1st attempt – 10 points

2nd attempt – 7 points

3rd attempt – 4 points

4th attempt or more – 1 point

IMPROVER DRILL

Skill Level: Advanced

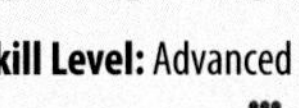

Group Size: 2-16

COPY CAT

This exercise is good for improving a climber's memory, focus, route reading and different styles of climbing.

Split the group into pairs. Ideally, each pair should contain climbers of similar abilities, but who favour different climbing styles.

Climber 1 gets to pick a route of their choice, and climb it slowly, with a slight pause after every movement. Climber 2 needs to observe, and try to remember the exact way that Climber 1 is climbing.

Once Climber 1 is back on the floor, Climber 2 attempts the route, climbing it in way that is as similar as possible to that of Climber 1. Once this is done, swap roles so that Climber 1 is watching, and Climber 2 is climbing first.

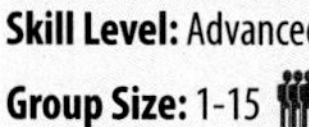

IMPROVER DRILL

●●●●

Skill Level: Advanced

Group Size: 1-15

CRIMP DRILL

This exercise helps climbers to learn crimping skills and strength.

If necessary, explain the difference between a half crimp and a full crimp. A half crimp is when the knuckles of your fingers are level with your finger tips. A full crimp is when your knuckles are higher than your finger tips.

Ask the climbers to climb a variety of crimpy routes. Whilst climbing, every time they reach a crimp they must initially hold it as a half crimp. From there, they have to turn it into a full crimp without letting go of the hold.

Repeat this process throughout the climb. A harder variation is to add a couple more steps for each crimp. For example, after they have a full crimp, they must return to a half crimp and then make their move.

IMPROVER DRILL

●●●●

Skill Level: Advanced

Group Size: 1-15

As a variation, include a core exercise such as **Three Knees Up** every time they cut loose.

CUT 1, 2, 3

This drill is perfect for improving a climber's core strength. It requires an overhang or roof area.

Pick a climb a couple of grades below the climber's normal level. Every time the climber moves a hand, they have to cut loose completely (feet come off the wall), count for 3 seconds, and then put their feet back onto the wall. Repeat this process on every move until the climb is complete.

IMPROVER DRILL

●●●●

Skill Level: Advanced

Group Size: 1-8

DIZZY CLIMBING

This exercise is useful for improving a climber's range of motion, core strength and roof climbing skills.

For this drill, you will need a cave or roof area with large holds where you can climb completely upside down. Have the climber get onto the roof with both feet on. Inform the climber that they must rotate 360° without cutting loose, or falling off. This means that they will have to really consider their footholds and reposition their hands as they rotate. It is a great way of introducing and teaching heel hooks, toe hooks and pinning of the feet.

IMPROVER DRILL

Skill Level: Advanced

Group Size: 1-20

This exercise works well when combined with the **Speed Climbing Drill** (page 87).

DYNAMIC FOOT SMEAR DRILL

The dynamic foot smear drill only really works once you have taught the dynamic foot smear technique (page 60).

This exercise is good for increasing a climber's overhang or vertical climbing ability. Choose a climb graded one or two grades below the climber's normal climbing level. Explain to the climber that they have to climb the route, but that they must include a dynamic foot smear as often as possible, potentially on every move!

IMPROVER DRILL

Skill Level: Advanced

Group Size: 1-4

FOOT SWAP ON BOARD

This exercise is perfect for climbers who are practising their foot swapping skills, especially on steep walls. It is also an extremely good core work out.

For this drill, you need access to a 40° board. Pick two wide handholds that are comfortable to hold but hard to move from.

Select a foothold quite low down, so the climber's knees are slightly bent. Then, simply have the climber perform a foot swap in both directions.

You can also be specific and pick a certain type of foot swap; for example, pick a hold big enough to perform a match footswap, and have them work primarily on that type of foot swap. Alternatively, the table-cloth foot swap is easy to practice in this drill.

IMPROVER DRILL

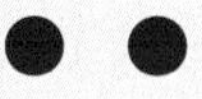

Skill Level: Advanced

Group Size: 1-4

A cool variation is to have the climbers pin and keep their foot on the selected hold for a few seconds.
Also, try the dynamic variation on page 114.

FOOT TAPS

This drill improves the climber's overhang climbing and foot-eye coordination, and helps them to practise pinning their feet. It is also a great core workout!

Have the climber deadhang on good holds on an overhanging wall. Point to a high hold out left, which the climber must touch with their left foot.

Immediately afterwards, point to a high hold out right; the climber must cut loose and tap this hold with their right foot. Repeat, varying the distance and height of holds, ensuring that the climber cuts loose between each tap.

IMPROVER DRILL

● ● ● ●

Skill Level: Advanced

Group Size: 1-4

97. FOOT TAPS (DYNAMIC)

A harder, more dynamic version of *Foot Taps* (page 113).

This is a really good drill for private tuitions or small groups. It also works well during group rotations.

This drill improves the climber's overhang climbing, foot-eye coordination, and helps them to practise pinning their feet. It is also a great core workout!

Ask the climber to deadhang on good holds on an overhanging wall. Point to a high hold out left which the climber must touch with their left foot.

Next, point to a foothold out right. The climber then has to swing and plant their right foot on your selected hold. However, they must do it in one swift motion.

Repeat, varying the distance and height of holds.

IMPROVER DRILL

Skill Level: Advanced

Group Size: 1-15

98. GOLF

This exercise is perfect for improving a climber's route reading, dynamic movement and deadpointing. It is also great for improving power endurance, as well as being a fun game.

Split the climbers into groups of 2 or 3, preferably of similar height and ability. Choose 6 or 7 climbs which you would normally expect them to flash easily. Each climb represents a hole, as if you were playing golf.

Start on the first climb, and explain to the climbers that the objective is to use as few holds as possible. For every hold the climber uses, they gain a point / stroke.

Each climber is only allowed to complete each climb once. If a climber falls off, they are allowed a second go, but must include the points from their last attempt.

Throughout the game, keep track of the scores. At the end of the game, the climber with the fewest points is the winner.

IMPROVER DRILL

Skill Level: Advanced

Group Size: 1-4

As a variation, try **Static Hand Taps** (below).

HAND TAPS (DYNAMIC)

This drill is good for improving a climber's dynamic climbing, power, and overhang climbing ability.

Find an overhanging wall with lots of holds. Ask the climber to get onto the wall, hanging on two handholds of their choice.

Point to a hold, and shout 'Left'. The climber must then pull up and tap the hold with their left hand dynamically, and catch their starting hold again, without touching the floor.

Next, shout 'Right' as you point to another hold. This time, the climber must pull up and tap the hold with their right hand, once again catching the starting hold on their way down.

IMPROVER DRILL

Skill Level: Advanced

Group Size: 1-4

As a variation, try **Dynamic Hand Taps** (above).

HAND TAPS (STATIC)

Another drill for improving a climber's static climbing, lock-off strength, and overhang climbing technique.

Find an overhanging wall with lots of holds. Ask the climber to get onto the wall, hanging on two handholds of their choice.

Point to a hold, and shout 'Left'. The climber then needs to pull up and lock their right arm, touch the hold with their left hand for two seconds, and then return to their starting hold. At no point are they allowed to touch the floor.

Next, shout 'Right' as you point to another hold. This time, the climber needs to lock off with their left arm and touch the hold for a few seconds with their right hand before returning to the starting hold.

Warm-Ups
Coordination
Techniques
Improver Drills
Group Management
Games
Team Building
Coaching
Resources
Recommended Drills

IMPROVER DRILL

Skill Level: Advanced

Group Size: 1-20

As a variation, try asking the climbers to hold a full lock, instead of 90°. Alternatively, try **Lock and Move** (page 117).

HOVER 90°

This drill is great for improving a climber's lock-off strength, body position and engagement of muscles. It is a much harder and more training-focused version of the *Hover Hands* drill (page 71).

Ask the climber to choose a route to climb. Every time the climber wishes to move a hand, they have to lock their other arm at 90° and hover their hand about an inch away from the hold for about 3 seconds.

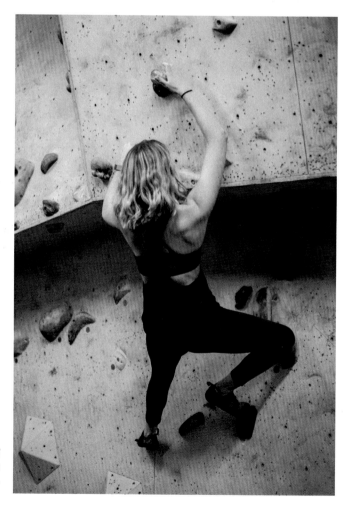

Hover Lock *– A simple and effective way to work on lock-off strength.*

IMPROVER DRILL

Skill Level: Advanced

Group Size: 1-20

HOVER LOCK AND MOVE

This is harder variation of *Hover 90°* (page 116), and is perfect for building a climber's strength and lock ability. I normally ban twisting, so each move is like a big rockover.

Ask the climber to choose a route to climb. Every time the climber wishes to move a hand, they have to lock their other arm at a full lock, hold for three seconds, lower down to a 90° lock, pause and pull back up to a full lock for another three seconds. Meanwhile, their other hand is hovering as close to the hold as possible, and is only allowed to grab it once the sequence is complete.

For example, if Mica wants to move her left hand onto the next hold, her right arm has to perform a full lock, and her left hand hovers as close to the hold as possible. After three seconds, Mica lowers down until her right arm is at a 90° lock, pauses for a moment, and pulls up to a full lock again, without the use of her left hand. After a further three seconds, her left hand can grab the hold.

IMPROVER DRILL

Skill Level: Advanced

Group Size: 1-16

Depending on their ability, you could encourage the climbers to campus back down too.

NO FEET

This strength-based exercise is excellent for teaching climbers how to campus and campus swing.

Ask the climbers to go and climb any overhanging or roof climbs of their choice. However, for the duration of this drill they are banned from using their feet at all, and are only allowed to campus.

IMPROVER DRILL

Skill Level: Advanced

Group Size: 2-14

PEER OBJECTIVES

Pick one of your more advanced climbers, and see if they can complete this challenge. You could add a reward – e.g. if they complete the challenge, they win a chocolate bar.

The climber has thirty minutes to achieve the objective, which is to take another climber (of a much lower standard) and help them reach a new grade that they have never climbed before.

At the end of the session, you can return the favour to the climbers who were coaching, by asking the other climbers to brush holds or encourage the more experienced climbers on a project.

IMPROVER DRILL

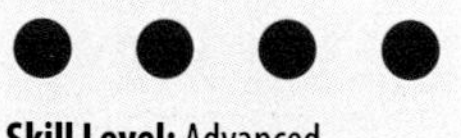

Skill Level: Advanced

Group Size: 1-15

PERFECT CLIMB

This drill is great for encouraging climbers to focus on honing their techniques. It is also good for route reading.

Explain to the climbers that they have twenty minutes to find a hard climb and complete every move. Next, they should repeat the same climb, focusing on getting every move just right.

Explain that the objective is to climb the route as efficiently as possible. Encourage them to focus on each move to determine the best possible technique. Make sure they are really precise on each move, analysing each one in detail – e.g. which foot swap would be better for this move?

It can also be effective to group climbers of the same ability together and have them try out each other's beta.

IMPROVER DRILL

Skill Level: Advanced

Group Size: 1-8

POINTS CONSTANT LADDER

This exercise is perfect for improving a climber's endurance and dynamic climbing, and for encouraging them to climb as quickly as possible. It is a much harder version of *Points Ladder* (page 119).

Have a list of your climbing wall's grading order, from lowest to highest (for example, grey, yellow, orange, purple, red, etc). Explain to the climbers that when you say 'Go', they must ladder their way up the grades. Everyone starts by climbing a grey problem, and as soon as they have finished the climb, they move on to a yellow problem.

However, they are not allowed to touch the floor between the climbs. If there isn't a climb near them that is within the grade range they need, they have to traverse until they find one.

If they fall off a climb, they must drop down a grade/colour. For example, if a climber falls off a purple, they go down to orange and start again from there.

Set a time, such as 15 minutes, and see who is on what colour when you stop the exercise.

IMPROVER DRILL

Skill Level: Advanced

Group Size: 1-8

POINTS LADDER

This exercise is ideal for improving a climber's endurance and dynamic climbing, and encouraging them to climb as quickly as possible.

Have a list of your climbing wall's grading order, from lowest to highest (for example, grey, yellow, orange, purple, red, etc). Explain to the climbers that when you say 'Go', they must ladder their way up the grades. Everyone starts by climbing a grey problem, and as soon as they have finished and reached the floor, they move on to a yellow problem.

If they fall off a climb, they drop down a grade/colour. For example, if a climber falls off a purple, they go down to orange and start again from there.

Set a time, such as 15 minutes, and see who is on what colour when you stop the exercise.

No repetition of routes – You can add a rule that they are not allowed to do the same climb twice. For example, if they drop down to orange, they have to pick a different orange instead of repeating the one they just did.

Personally, I like to have the no repeating routes rule up to a certain colour, e.g. red. So, if they have to repeat anything below a red, they are not allowed to do the same route. If they have to climb another red or a colour graded above red, they are allowed to repeat that climb.

Points system – You can also add a points system to inspire some healthy competition. For example, once they have reached and completed a white, they then have to climb a second white. If they manage to do so, they get their first point. If they do a third white in a row, they get a second point, and so on.

IMPROVER DRILL

Skill Level: Advanced

Group Size: 1-8

POINTS RACE

This exercise is perfect for improving a climber's endurance and dynamic climbing, and encouraging them to climb as quickly as possible.

Designate each colour or grade a point. For example, use the following format:

V1 = 1 point, V2 = 2 points, V3 = 3 points, etc.

Explain to the climbers that they need to reach a goal (e.g. 30 points) as quickly as they can. The first one to reach the target is the winner. The climbers can choose any combination of graded routes to reach the points target.

IMPROVER DRILL

Skill Level: Advanced

Group Size: 1-16

RACE GAME

This is a good drill to encourage climbers to move dynamically. It is also an excellent way of keeping training fun.

Ask everyone to sit down in a line in front of the wall, a few metres back. Explain to the climbers that you are going to pick two names from the group, and then you are going to shout 'Go'. The named climbers then have to get up and race to the top of the wall. Depending on their ability, you can either let them use any holds, or suggest a minimum colour / graded route.

The first one to the top has to do ten push-ups, and the climber who is second has to do fifteen. Repeat this drill choosing different climbers, and different exercises.

IMPROVER DRILL

Skill Level: Advanced

Group Size: 1-20

RECOGNITION

This is a really bizarre drill that I invented; I think it is perfect for something like a competition squad, or a group of people who have been training hard recently.

Begin by explaining that, as with most sports, it's hard to notice or recognise your improvement in climbing.

A climber who climbs V2 is desperate for their first V3. When the climber gets the V3, they aren't entirely happy, because they think it's a soft V3, and they want to get a second one. When they do, they aren't entirely happy, because it probably suited them and they want to be a proper V3 climber. Before you know it, the climber is climbing V3, but is unhappy because they are desperate to get their first V4.

Explain that you feel it is important to stop every now and again and recognise what you have achieved through your training.

Ask the group to split into pairs and sit on the floor. Make sure they are spread out, so that the pairs are not too close together.

One person in each pair should tell the other person something climbing-related that they are proud of having achieved in the last few months. They might say, 'I did my first 6b!' or 'I hit 1–4 on the campus board for the first time,' or 'I feel like I've got more dynamic in my climbing!'

After a minute, ask the other person to take their turn and say what they are proud of.

IMPROVER DRILL

Skill Level: Advanced

Group Size: 5-20

RED FLAG STYLE

I learnt this drill from Kris Peters at the BMC Coaching Symposium, and absolutely loved it! It is only suitable for advanced climbers, and is nicknamed a Reg Flag as it is very challenging. Be prepared for it to take up an entire session.

Tell the group that they are going to jog on the spot. You are going to shout out an exercise (e.g. push-ups), and everyone must complete it. As soon as each climber has finished, they stand up and jog on the spot again. Once everyone has finished and is jogging on the spot, you are going to shout out another exercise (e.g. leg raises), and repeat this process.

Explain that after 8-10 different exercises, you are going to shout 'Go'. From the moment you shout 'Go', they have thirty seconds to have some water, and ten minutes to go and complete their climbing task.

The task is for each climber to complete four easy climbs and two hard climbs. Climbers are allowed up to four attempts per hard climb.

Easy climb – An easy climb should be the hardest climb or colour they think they can flash in their current state. It can't be too easy.

Hard climb – A hard climb should be a climb that they think they can finish on their third or fourth attempt. If they can't do the first few moves, it's too hard. If they come off the last move on their third go – perfect!

Explain that they need to manage their time themselves, and when there are 30 seconds left, they need to be back in the training area and jogging on the spot.

That is the end of round one. I aim to complete four rounds in total, increasing the quantity of exercise reps each round. Example exercises are shown below:

Round One	Round Two	Round Three	Round Four
10 push-ups	15 push-ups	20 push-ups	25 push-ups
10 shoulder taps	15 shoulder taps	20 shoulder taps	25 shoulder taps
15 crunches	20 crunches	25 crunches	30 crunches
15 leg raises	20 leg raises	25 leg raises	30 leg raises
6 squat jumps	8 squat jumps	10 squat jumps	12 squat jumps
10 push-ups	15 push-ups	20 push-ups	25 push-ups
10 v-sits	15 v-sits	20 v-sits	25 v-sits

IMPROVER DRILL

Skill Level: Advanced

Group Size: 1-5

ROOF CUT LOOSE

This exercise is perfect for improving a climber's ability to cut loose (purposely release their feet from the wall).

Have the climber deadhang on a jug in a roof or cave area. Explain that you are going to push the climber's body, so that they become a big pendulum. They then have to bring their knees up, tuck their elbows in and stop swinging entirely.

Once they have stopped the swing, either repeat the exercise or move onto a different hold.

IMPROVER DRILL

Skill Level: Advanced

Group Size: 1-4

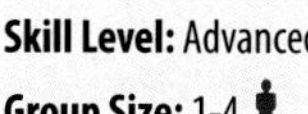

ROOF HEEL-TOE MATCH

This drill is good for improving a climber's roof climbing ability, heel hooks, toe hooks, bat hangs and foot swaps.

Ask the climbers find some good handholds in a roof or cave area, and pull on so both feet are on the wall, and the climber is upside down.

Choose a big, juggy hold for a left heel hook as their starting position. Explain to the climbers that the aim is to release their left heel hook, and replace it with a left toe hook.

To do this, have them toe hook the same hold with their right foot, then change their left foot from a heel hook to a toe hook. This will enable them to then release their right toe hook and return it to the starting position, ready to repeat. If they cut loose, they must start again.

IMPROVER DRILL

Skill Level: Advanced

Group Size: 1-15

As a variation, try **Roof Pinning** (page 124) in the same session.

ROOF HOOKING

This is a great drill for climbers who are practising their heel hooks and toe hooks. It is also great for improving a climber's roof-climbing ability.

Explain to the climbers that they must climb in the roof or cave area. They can either try a route of their choice, or use any colour for their feet. The objective is to practise all types of hooks.

Explain that the climbers should climb their chosen route but they are only allowed to use heel hooks or toe hooks for their feet.

If they cut loose at all, they have to start again.

IMPROVER DRILL

Skill Level: Advanced

Group Size: 1-4

ROOF PINNING

This is a useful drill to improve a climber's roof-climbing ability, and the technique of pulling in with their feet. It is also good for optimising their core engagement. I usually do this drill after teaching *Pulling in With Feet* (page 60).

For this exercise you'll need a roof or cave area. Climbers can either try a route of their choice, or use any colour for their feet. The objective is to practise pinning holds with the feet, rather than simply to get up the climb. Explain that the climbers have to climb their route, but that they are only allowed to pull down with the toes; heel hooks, toe hooks, twisting and flagging are banned. If they cut loose at all, they have to start again.

Be sure that they engage their foot and pin the hold before they let go with their hands. Be aware of their foot position too – on a roof they will need some upwards pull on the footholds.

IMPROVER DRILL

Skill Level: Advanced

Group Size: 1-20

ROUTE-READING ANALYSIS

A great drill for encouraging climbers to route read, and to analyse their route-reading strengths and weaknesses.

Split the group into pairs and ask them to choose a route to climb. Before Climber 1 climbs, they have to mark down their route on a sheet of paper and map out how they plan to climb it. For example, a climber might write: '*Start matched, left hand to crimp, right hand to sloper, match, right hand again.*'

Once they have finished planning their route, Climber 2 films Climber 1 as they climb their route. Then let them watch the video and check through their notes to see if they climbed it as planned. Discuss why moves were different – for example, did they not consider matching originally?

For experienced climbers, note down foot movements too, including flagging and edge types.

IMPROVER DRILL

Skill Level: Advanced

Group Size: 1-15

ROUTE-READING DISCUSSION

This drill is perfect for experienced climbers trying to hone their route-reading skills before a competition.

Simply walk around the centre and analyse different routes, discussing each climber's beta. Discuss tricks such as looking at how holds have been chalked up. Another tip is to look out for dirty parts of holds, which can show where a lot of people have stood in the past, normally indicating the best part of the hold.

Also discuss grippy places to smear – a lot of indoor climbing wall panels are really slippery, with a few bits of dot showing the remaining parts of sticky paint, which also provide the most friction for smearing.

IMPROVER DRILL

Skill Level: Advanced

Group Size: 1-6

Make the setters think more by adding extra rules. You could specify that people lose 20 points for failing to complete a problem they have set, or perhaps tell them that they are not allowed to test their problem or touch the wall during their setting.

SETTING PROBLEMS

Route-setting is very technical, and improves your route-reading skills. It is similar to climbing in the sense that you have to consider multiple factors, and is a good problem-solving exercise.

Depending on the group size, either split the group into pairs or have them work as individuals. Explain that the task involves each of them setting one or two boulder problems. Once the climbs have been set, have a mini competition between the climbers using the problems that they set.

IMPROVER DRILL

Skill Level: Advanced

Group Size: 1-10

Campus Add-On (page 110) is a fun game to play after this drill. It also works well in the same session as **Swing Challenge** (below).

STRAIGHT ARM CAMPUS

This drill is perfect for improving a climber's campus-swing technique (page 58).

Select low-grade routes with lots of jugs on a relatively steep wall.

Explain to the climbers that they need to climb by campusing only. However, the climbers must campus without bending their arms at all. Encourage climbers to generate momentum by swinging their hips and legs back and forth as required.

IMPROVER DRILL

Skill Level: Advanced

Group Size: 1-10

I normally do this exercise in the same session as the **Straight Arm Campus** drill (above), and follow it up with **Swing Square** (page 126).

SWING CHALLENGE

This is an amazing drill that improves a climber's campus swing ability (page 58) and coordination.

Find a roof or cave area with lots of big handholds. Explain to the climbers that they need to start by dead-hanging on the jugs, and then jump their feet as far forward as possible.

Encourage them to gain as much momentum as possible by swinging their hips and legs to and fro. After their attempt, mark their landing spots and then ask them to try and beat their markers.

IMPROVER DRILL

Skill Level: Advanced

Group Size: 1-10

This exercise works well in the same session as teaching the **Campus Swing** (page 58). It also works well after **Swing Challenge** (above), and can be followed by a **Straight Arm Campus** drill (above.)

SWING SQUARE

This is a harder variation of *Swing Challenge* (above), which introduces more coordination and accuracy.

Find a roof with lots of big handholds. Place squares and lines of tape onto the floor, 3 -5ft in front of the jugs.

Explain to the climbers that they need to start by dead-hanging on the jugs, and then swing and jump onto a specific square or line of tape that you designate. You could, for example, use different coloured tape and ask climbers to swing into a specific coloured square. Encourage them to gain as much momentum as they need by swinging their hips and legs. After their attempt, pick a different square or line for them to aim for.

As a variation, you could introduce a second move. For example once they have landed on a blue square they must squat jump immediately to a red square about a metre away.

IMPROVER DRILL

Skill Level: Advanced

Group Size: 1-15

TEACHING

Teaching is a great exercise for tactfully reinforcing techniques and building a climber's confidence.

By using this drill multiple sessions in a row with my competition squad, we managed to revisit and cycle through all of our techniques again in a new and fun way.

Split the group into teams of three. Give each team a different technique to teach the rest of the group. For example, Team 1 could teach everyone how to smear.

Send the teams away and give them fifteen minutes in which to prepare a small presentation to teach their technique. Also request that each team runs a new drill for their technique that both the coaches and the team have never seen before.

During their preparation time, be sure to walk around and guide each team towards the key points using leading questions. For example, if Team 1 is covering smearing, ask them some questions like, 'How high should you smear?', 'What should your knee be doing?', 'What about your rubber?'

After the designated time, call in the groups. Begin with the first team's presentation and get everyone to test out their new drill. Then move on to the next team's presentation.

You may wish to add a question and answer session at the end of each presentation.

IMPROVER DRILL

Skill Level: Advanced

Group Size: 1-15

TEAM PRESSURE

This drill is only for the advanced climbers who are competing on a regular basis. I did this drill with my squad before a big competition, to try to manage their anxiety and nerves.

Explain to the climbers that the aim of this drill is to put them under pressure at the same time as training. Begin by asking the group to do a sequence of exercises. I normally go for ten push-ups, ten crunches, ten leg raises and ten squat jumps. Once they have finished, explain that this sequence of exercises will be a forfeit.

Next, guide the group to a random wall and select a climber from the team to attempt a particular climb; if they fall off, the entire team has to do the sequence of exercises. This works best if you pick climbs just below the climber's crux grade. Be sure to explain to the group that they are a team, and that you expect lots of encouragement from the group.

It also works well to pick climbs that are too hard, redefining the third or fourth hold as a target. If the climber hits the target, then the team doesn't need to do their exercises.

Once the climber has completed their attempt, choose a different climb and a different climber. Make sure that the targets are realistic so that you can have four or five climbers in a row complete a climb successfully.

You can also include specific techniques within this drill; for example, climb a blue route smearing only.

IMPROVER DRILL

Skill Level: Advanced

Group Size: 1-4

TECHNIQUE ANALYSIS

This training-based drill is perfect for getting climbers to practise all of the techniques that you have covered.

Allocate some routes to the climbers and explain that they should climb them using all of their techniques, as fluently as possible. Explain that for every mistake you notice, they will have to do three tricep push-ups. For example, if you have taught the climber how to foot swap, and they chose to use a really risky foot swap, penalise them three push-ups.

Always be sure to explain what they did incorrectly and how it could be improved. Keep an eye out for bad foot placements, body positioning, route-reading, flags, and anything else that you might have covered in training sessions.

IMPROVER DRILL

Skill Level: Advanced

Group Size: 1-15

A really challenging combination for advanced climbers is to combine this drill with **No Foot Swapping** (page 73).

TECH FLAGS ONLY

This exercise is useful for improving a climber's understanding of technical flags.

This exercise only works on vertical or overhanging climbs. Ask the climbers to climb a route graded slightly below their normal climbing ability. Explain that for every move they need to be in perfect balance, and perform a flag on the correct side. However, they are not allowed to do a normal flag – they can only do technical flags (inside or back flags).

IMPROVER DRILL

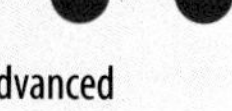

Skill Level: Advanced

Group Size: 1-16

TIRED CORE

This training-based drill is a great core workout, and is also useful for showing climbers how much we use our core whilst we climb.

Get the climbers to do a ten-minute core workout to get their core tired. Straight after this, send them off climbing. Before they attempt a climb, however, they must do ten V-sits immediately before getting onto the wall. They should repeat this before every attempt at a climb, and you should ensure that they don't have time to rest in between their V-sits and their attempt.

IMPROVER DRILL

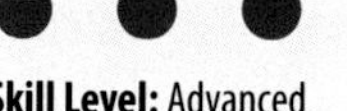

Skill Level: Advanced

Group Size: 1-20

WINDMILL DRILL

This exercise is a fun drill, perfect for teaching climbers to windmill and to weight a hold correctly. This can be critical when trying to match on a sloper.

Have the climbers climb either at, or one grade below, their normal climbing level. Every time they move a hand, they have to first move it below the hold that they are releasing. For example, if they have their right hand on a hold at shoulder height, when they release their hand it has to go closer to the floor before gaining any height.

With big rockover moves, or awkward slabby routes, have them exaggerate a windmill by throwing their arm in a circle, starting low and coming all the way up and away from their body.

Get them to drop an arm and repeat this process during every move they make.

IMPROVER DRILL

Skill Level: Advanced

Group Size: 1-16

YO-YOs

This exercise is perfect for climbers working on their route-reading and endurance or power endurance.

Pick a boulder problem that is easily doable, but slightly challenging for the climber.

The climber has to make the first move of the problem, and then reverse the move back to the starting position. Next, without coming off the wall, they must complete the first two moves, and then reverse back to the starting position again.

Repeat this process until they have reached the top of the climb.

From there, they must climb down the route, but reverse the process, climbing back up to the top for every move.

GROUP MANAGEMENT DRILLS

The drills described in this chapter are exercises to improve a climber's ability, predominantly aimed at younger age groups. These drills also help to improve and maintain an instructor's group management skills.

Some of the drills are game-based, and others cover a wide range of techniques.

An ideal age range and group size is suggested for each drill, although these are very much at the instructor's discretion – it may be perfectly possible to teach younger climbers drills recommended for older children, and vice versa. Drills are arranged in alphabetical order.

GROUP MANAGEMENT DRILL

5 6 7 8 9 10 11 12 13 14 15 16

Age Range: 5-9

Group Size: 2-15

1. BEANBAG FETCH

This exercise is perfect for younger climbers who are still building confidence.

Split the climbers into pairs and give them a beanbag per pair. The first climber climbs up a wall of their choice, whilst carrying the beanbag. They are not allowed to cheat by carrying the beanbag in their mouths or putting it in their pockets.

The climber climbs with the beanbag to a height at which they feel comfortable, then leaves it on a hold of their choice before climbing back down.

The second climber then climbs up to the beanbag, and has to carry it down (again, without using their teeth, pockets, etc) until they reach the floor. It is then their turn to place the beanbag on the wall in the same way.

GROUP MANAGEMENT DRILL

5 6 7 8 9 10 11 12 13 14 15 16

Age Range: 7-12

Group Size: 2-8

2. BLINDFOLD NINJA

This exercise is perfect for encouraging climbers to use quiet feet.

Choose either one or two walls as the designated area for this activity. Explain to the climbers that all but one person will be on the wall at the same time. The climber who isn't on the wall will be blindfolded, and will have to find the climbers.

The blindfolded climber is not allowed to look, so can only listen for noisy climbers. It's wise to have a height restriction, and to avoid climbers climbing above each other.

GROUP MANAGEMENT DRILL

5 6 7 8 9 10 11 12 13 14 15 16

Age Range: 10-16

Group Size: 2-10

3. BLINDFOLD TAGS

More of a game than a drill, this is a fun way of improving endurance, route-reading and much more.

Choose a strip of wall about ten metres long. Have a starting hold and a finishing hold, and a designated hold in the middle. Put red rugby tags and blue rugby tags on different holds across the wall.

Split the group up into two teams, with one team starting on the left and the other team starting on the right. Explain to the climbers that they will start at the beginning, and climb until they reach the designated central hold.

Along the way, if they knock off a red tag they lose a point. If they successfully grab a blue tag and place it on their belt, they gain two points. However, the climbers will be blindfolded throughout.

You can also run this activity without teams, making it more of a team-building experience than a competitive game.

Explain that this is not a race, but that the team with the most points when everyone has traversed will be the winning team.

If you don't have rugby tags then corks or beanbags work equally well.

GROUP MANAGEMENT DRILL

5 6 7 8 9 10 11 12 13 14 15 16

Age Range: 5-9

Group Size: 3-20

4. BUDDY CHECKS

Once you have introduced the *Safety Triangle* (page 137), it is a good idea to include the buddy check system, with some bouldering climbing calls.

Having some form of structure and giving each individual a role will encourage good behaviour and help to prevent children from running around.

Explain that before the climber starts climbing, they have to complete their 'buddy checks'. The climber starts by turning to the buddy responsible for encouraging and asks, 'Ready to encourage?' Their friend replies by saying, 'I'm ready!'

The climber then turns to the buddy responsible for keeping the triangle safe and asks, 'Ready to keep everyone out of the triangle?' The other person replies by saying, 'I'm ready!'

The climber is then free to climb.

GROUP MANAGEMENT DRILL

5 6 7 8 9 10 11 12 13 14 15 16

Age Range: 5-16

Group Size: 1-30

5. CLIMBING!

This exercise is simply organised climbing. I include it here as it is my go-to exercise when I have a large group.

Split the climbers into groups of 2 to 4, and have a designated station for each climb. You could use beanbags to mark the stations.

Place each group in front of their designated climb. If necessary, assign roles to each group member to help with group management – for example the *Safety Triangle drill* (page 137).

Give the climbers one go per climb and then rotate around the stations. I often call the climbers together for a quick technique chat in between station rotations, and send them away with simple drills and exercises.

GROUP MANAGEMENT DRILL

5 6 7 8 9 10 11 12 13 14 15 16

Age Range: 10-16

Group Size: 4-10

6. GETTING DRESSED

This exercise is great for experienced climbers looking to improve their body positioning and foot placements.

Have items of clothing hung up on holds on a wall. Ask the climbers to climb a route – either let them use any coloured holds or choose an easy route. Every time they pass an item of clothing, they have to put it on whilst they are still on the wall.

This activity also works well in two teams, a point being awarded to the team whose climber finishes the route first, wearing all of the collected clothing.

Some suggestions for clothing items include gloves, hats, sunglasses, scarf, socks, etc.

GROUP MANAGEMENT DRILL

5 6 7 8 9 10 11 12 13 14 15 16

Age Range: 10-16

Group Size: 4-12

Depending on group size and ability, this can also be run as an individual exercise.

7. LONG TRAVERSING GAME

Choose a stretch of wall and lay a rope down on the floor in the shape of a semi-circle, linking the start of the wall to the end of the wall.

Split the group into pairs, with three or four feet of rope connecting them (they can do this by tucking the end of the rope into their trousers). They must then traverse the wall in their pairs, and walk back along the rope leading to the start of the wall, where they start again.

Each team has three lives, and loses a life every time their rope is dropped or a team member falls off.

Add additional variations or challenges during the course of the game, such as the following:

Tennis Ball **–** Give each team a tennis ball which they have to carry with them, without putting it in their pockets. Every time you say switch, they have to pass the tennis ball to their team member. If they drop the ball or fall off, they lose a point.

Pack of Cards **-** Lay out a pack of cards on the floor next to the wall. Every time a team climbs past the cards, they have to pick up a card of your choice. If they fall off, they lose a point.

Chalk Board **-** Lay a chalkboard on the mats next to the wall. Every time a team passes the chalkboard, they have to write their name. If they fall off, they lose a point.

GROUP MANAGEMENT DRILL

5 6 7 8 9 10 11 12 13 14 15 16

Age Range: 5-12

Group Size: 1-20

I often introduce this activity shortly after trying the **Stop! 1, 2, 3!** exercise (page 75).

8. ITCHY HEAD

This exercise is a variation of the drill *Hover*, but is better suited for the younger ages. It is perfect for climbers who are practising flagging, and also works well as a warm-up activity.

Ask the climbers to choose a route to climb. Every time the climber wishes to move a hand, they have to scratch their head for a couple of seconds before grabbing their next hold.

If the climber is in a bad position, with a chance of barn-dooring, they will lose energy, struggle and potentially fall off. This exercise therefore forces them to consider their body positioning and the need for flagging.

GROUP MANAGEMENT DRILL

5 6 7 8 9 10 11 12 13 14 15 16

Age Range: 5-9

Group Size: 3-20

9. SAFETY TRIANGLE

This is not really a drill, but more of a group management technique to control a large group of young children. It can be applied to any drill or exercise that involves climbing on the wall.

Split the climbers into groups of three, and have them stand in a triangle, with one person standing in front of the climb.

The first person will be climbing (or carrying out whatever the set task is). The second person, who is standing back and right, is responsible for encouragement and advice. The third person, who is standing back and left, is responsible for keeping the triangle shape and not letting anyone, apart from an instructor, enter the triangle.

GAMES

In this chapter I have suggested some fun activities, perfect for birthday parties or for the end of a session.

The list is arranged in alphabetical order, and for each game I have suggested a suitable age range and group size. This is, of course, just a guide, and is subject to the abilities of the group and instructor preference – make your own judgement on which games will suit your group.

GAME

13 14 15 16

Age Range: 13-16

Group Size: 2-20

1. BLINDFOLD TAG GAME

Choose a strip of wall about 10 metres long. Designate a starting hold at both the left and right ends, and a finishing hold in the middle of the wall. Put red rugby tags and blue rugby tags on different holds across the wall.

Split the group into two teams, with Team 1 starting from the left and Team 2 starting from the right. In each round, one climber from each team will be blindfolded. They will start from their own side, and climb until they reach the middle hold, picking up blue tags as they go. For each blue tag they collect, they will receive two points, but for each red tag that they knock off, they will lose a point.

Explain that it is not a race – the winning team will be the team with the most points after everyone has climbed.

GAME

13 14 15 16

Age Range: 13-16

Group Size: 8-30

2. CLIMBING DODGE BALL

Line the players up, facing the wall, on a line a metre or so away from the wall. Have a second line around three metres behind them.

Choose a keyword for each game, for example 'it'. Every time you say the keyword, the players must touch the second line and then get onto the wall as quickly as they can, with both feet off the floor. If you touch them with the ball while they are doing this, they are out. They must line up again after each round.

GAME

5 6 7 8 9 10 11 12 13 14 15 16

Age Range: 5-16

Group Size: 6-20

A useful additional rule is to say that people are not allowed to cross the line until you say 'Go'. This is a good way of stopping people from running before you've finished your sentence.

3. COACH SAYS

A climbing version of the popular kids' party game, *Simon Says*. In this version, each command should be climbing-related.

All the climbers start behind a line. If you say, "Coach says 'grey holds only'," the climbers must get onto the wall using grey holds only, with both feet off the floor. The last person to successfully obey the command is out. If you do not begin your command with 'Coach says...', a climber will be out if they cross the line.

GAME

5 6 7 8 9 10 11 12 13 14 15 16

Age Range: 5-16

Group Size: 4-20

4. CLIMBING TWISTER

All the climbers start on the wall. Shout out the colour of a hold and which hand or foot they must touch it with. For example, 'Left hand orange.'

They must then manoeuvre until their left hand is on an orange hold. If they fail to do this, or fall off in the process, they are out!

Repeat until there is only one climber left.

GAME

5 6 7 8 9 10 11 12 13 14 15 16

Age Range: 5-16

Group Size: 3-20

5. DEAD-HANG CHALLENGE

Choose a designated area of the climbing wall. Give the climbers 30 seconds to get on the wall, during which they can go anywhere within the designated area.

By the end of the 30 seconds, they must all be on the wall, hanging from their arms with both feet off the floor, but not using any footholds.

From now on, if their feet touch the floor, they are out. The last person left hanging on the wall is the winner.

GAME

5 6 7 8 9 10 11 12 13 14 15 16

Age Range: 5-16

Group Size: 3-20

6. HANG TOUGH

The game works the same way as *Dead Hang Challenge*, but you can set additional challenges for the climbers while they are hanging on the wall.

Examples could include:

- The climbers must put one foot above their head.
- The climbers must touch the floor with one hand.
- The climbers must clap their hands twice without falling off.

GAME

5 6 7 8 9

Age Range: 5-9

Group Size: 8-25

7. MOUNTAIN VALLEY CAVE

Choose a strip of wall. The left half of the wall is the Mountain, the right side of the wall is the Cave, and the area in front of the wall is the Valley.

The climbers must jog or cycle in the Valley until you shout a command.

If you shout 'Mountain', the climbers must get onto the left side of the wall as quickly as possible. The last person to get on the wall is out.

Depending on the age of the group members, add additional rules to spice it up. For example, if you shout 'Jump!' they must spin around. If you shout 'Spin!' they have to jump.

GAME

5 6 7 8 9

Age Range: 5-9

Group Size: 8-25

If you don't have a way to control music, then you can just shout 'Freeze' and 'Continue' instead.

8. MUSICAL CLIMBERS

This game is similar to *Musical Chairs* or *Musical Statues*. You will need a speaker or remote control of the wall's music system.

The climbers start on the wall. Every time the music stops, the climbers must stay completely still, regardless of what position they are in. If a climber falls off, or moves in any way while the music is not playing, they are out.

GAME

5 6 7 8 9

Age Range: 5-9

Group Size: 1-15

9. NOODLE OBSTACLES

Before the session starts, set up some noodle holders in various positions across the wall. Have some noodles positioned in a way that forces you to climb through them, and also include half noodles sticking out like a limbo bars which climbers must climb above or below.

The climbers must climb through and around the obstacles, without knocking the noodles off the wall.

GAME

10 11 12 13 14 15 16

Age Range: 10-16

Group Size: 6-12

10. RELAY RACE

Choose a strip of wall about 10 metres long, with designated holds at the left and right ends, as well as one in the middle.

Split the group into two teams and give them 30 seconds to decide on a team name and a team order.

Team 1 starts at the left end of the wall. Team 2 starts at the right end of the wall. When you shout 'Go', the first member of each team must start traversing towards the middle. When they reach the middle hold, they jump off and the next member of their team starts climbing.

If a climber falls off, they must get back on the wall wherever they were when they fell off. The winning team is the first team to have all climbers touch the middle hold.

GAME

10 11 12 13 14 15 16

Age Range: 10-16

Group Size: 3-10

11. ROCK WARRIORS

Choose a strip of wall about 10 metres long, with designated holds at the left and right ends, as well as one in the middle.

Choose 3 or 4 climbers to get on the wall, an equal distance apart. When you shout 'Go', they must climb to their left until they reach the finishing hold. They then jump off the wall, run back to the starting hold, and get back on the wall.

If the climber falls, they must wait 3 seconds before getting back onto the wall. If a climber catches a climber in front of them and touches them, that climber is out.

The game continues until there is only one person left.

GAME

5 6 7 8 9 10 11 12 13 14 15 16

Age Range: 5-16

Group Size: 3-30

A popular variation is **Baby Sharks**, in which once you catch somebody they also become a shark.

12. SHARK ATTACK

Mark out a large area close to the wall, with a border 4 to 6 metres back. This area is the ocean. When you shout 'Swim!' the climbers must walk around in the ocean, pretending to swim.

When you shout 'Shark Attack!', the climbers must touch the border at the edge of the ocean and then get onto the wall as quickly as possible.

If you manage to grab a climber before they get onto the wall, they are out.

GAME

10 11 12 13 14 15 16

Age Range: 10-16

Group Size: 6-12

CAUTION! – This game can be dangerous. Participants should be warned that they are not allowed to kick their opponent!

13. SOCK WRESTLING

This game requires a high beam, two harnesses, two slings and two carabiners. Attach the slings around the beam, and connect a carabiner to each sling.

Ask two climbers to put on a harness on back to front, so that their belay loop is behind them.

Use a chair to attach the carabiner on a sling to the belay loop of a climber. Once you have both climbers attached they should be hanging facing the floor, but unable to reach it.

Explain to the climbers that the winner is the first person to take a sock off their opponent's foot.

Get In Touch

KENT & SUSSEX CLIMBING

MASTERS SQUAD

JUNIOR SQUAD

PARA SQUAD

info@ksclimbing.co.uk  @knsclimbing ksclimbing.co.uk

SEAA
ENGLAND
20
18
ROAD RELAY
CHAMPIONSHIPS
DEPOT
CLIMBING
JINGLE
BELLS
KENT &
SUSSEX
CLIMBING
SUSSEX
CLIMBING

CHAPTER 7

TEAM BUILDING

Team-building exercises can be very useful if you are trying to create a bond in any form of group or team. This can be particularly important in a climbing squad.

Obviously, climbing gets priority, but creating a fun and social environment helps you to motivate and get the most out of participants.

Some of these team-building exercises are also great warm-up activities, and work well as ice-breakers at the start of a session.

TEAM BUILDING

7 8 9 10 11 12 13 14 15 16

Age Range: 7-16

Group Size: 5-15

1. ANIMAL SOUNDS

This exercise is a brilliant warm-up exercise when trying to build a team bond in a group such as a climbing squad.

Explain to everyone that they are going to be given an animal to mimic. Once they have their animal, they are no longer allowed to talk or tell anyone what animal they are; instead, they can only make the noise that their animal would make. For example, if a climber is asked to mimic a dog, they are only allowed to bark.

Once everyone has been given an animal to mimic, they have to arrange themselves in order from the smallest animal to the biggest animal.

Some good animal suggestions are: bee, snake, duck, dinosaur, sheep, cow, hamster, etc.

TEAM BUILDING

10 11 12 13 14 15 16

Age Range: 10-16

Group Size: 8-20

2. CHEMICAL SPILL

This bonding exercise is great for building communication skills.

Lay out a rope in the shape of a circle, with about a 3 metre radius. Place a container or bucket in the middle with a little bit of water inside. It is important that the container has a lip at the top. Also lay out different lengths of rope outside of the area.

Inform the team that toxic chemicals are leaking out of the container, and that the issue needs to be resolved. The circled area is contaminated and deadly, and no one can step into it.

The team's task is to remove the container from the area and into safety. However, there are a few important rules:

1. The bucket cannot be dragged, only lifted.

2. No one is allowed inside the contaminated area.

3. If any piece of equipment touches the floor in the area, it can't be used anymore, as it is contaminated.

If you wish to encourage the naturally quiet members to lead, blindfold the natural leaders.

Youth climbing squad – Training is most effective when it's fun!

TEAM BUILDING

10 11 12 13 14 15 16

Age Range: 10-16

Group Size: 5-20

3. COMPUTER VIRUS

This is another good bonding exercise for building communication skills.

Form a circled area with a 20 metre rope. Inside the area, place sheets of paper, each with a letter of the alphabet, one for each letter. Lay the letters out in a random order, but don't place any of them on top of another.

Inform the team that there is a computer virus that is going to destroy the world, and that they are the only people who can save the world. The circled area is the only computer that can delete the virus.

To delete the virus, they have to enter the code. The code is a word or sentence with the same number of letters as the number of people in the group (for example, if you have 15 people, you need a 15 letter code). To enter the code, they need to enter the circle, and place a foot (sometimes a specific foot) on the button.

However, there are a few really important rules:

1. They only have one attempt at entering the code.

2. Only one person is allowed to enter the circle at a time.

3. Each person has to stand on at least one letter.

4. They have five minutes to plan, and two minutes to enter the code.

TEAM BUILDING

7 8 9 10 11 12 13 14 15 16

Age Range: 7-16

Group Size: 8-20

4. HELIUM STICK

This is an interesting team bonding exercise. A good learning objective is to not blame each other.

Ask the climbers to get into two lines, facing each other, with their arms out straight and their index fingers pointing away from themselves. Rest a long thin stick (such as a bamboo cane or tent pole) across everyone's index fingers. Ask everyone to adjust their arms until the stick is level, and explain that they can only hold the stick with their index fingers.

The objective is to lower the stick down onto the floor. However, there are a few rules:

1. Everybody's index finger must remain in contact with the stick at all times.

2. No one is allowed to pinch or grab the stick; it can only rest on top of their fingers.

3. If anyone's finger is caught not making contact with the stick, they have to start again.

TEAM BUILDING

5 6 7 8 9 10 11 12 13 14 15 16

Age Range: 5-16

Group Size: 8-20

5. HUMAN TWISTER

This is a perfect warm-up exercise when trying to build a team bond in a group such as a climbing squad.

Ask everyone to stand in a circle facing inwards. Ask everyone to put their right hand forward and link hands with someone random across the circle.

Next, ask everyone to stick their left hand up and grab onto the left hand of someone else.

It is really important that they don't grab the same person's hand twice. It is also important that no one holds the hand of someone who is right next to them.

The objective of this task is to untangle themselves without unlinking hands. If the chain is broken, they have to start the task again.

TEAM BUILDING

10 11 12 13 14 15 16

Age Range: 10-16

Group Size: 8-20

6. MINUTE CIRCLE

This bonding exercise is useful for building communication skills.

Lay out a rope in the shape of a circle, about the size of a hula hoop. Inform the team that when you say 'Go', you will start the stopwatch. When the team thinks a minute has elapsed, they have to place one foot on the rope.

Explain that the objective is to have the entire team place one foot on the rope at exactly the same time. If they fail to do so, they have to start again.

Naturally, they will focus on the time, and try to get as close to the minute as they can. However, the objective of this task is to place their feet on the rope at the same time. This exercise requires some careful and precise wording.

TEAM BUILDING

10 11 12 13 14 15 16

Age Range: 10-16

Group Size: 9-25

7. ROBOT WARS

This exercise is good for building communication skills within your squad.

Set out an area smaller than a five-a-side football pitch. Lay out some soft footballs (minimum of ten) across the floor.

Divide the group into teams of three. One person per team is the robot, whose job is to pick up the balls and throw them at the other robots. Every time the robot hits another robot, they get a point. However, the robot is blindfolded.

The other two team members are controllers and must stand, facing each other, on the edge of the area so that one controller has their back to the area.

The controller who is facing the area, and can see the robot, is not allowed to speak. The controller with their back to the area is allowed to speak.

The first team to reach three points is the winner. Give the teams two minutes for planning, in which they must come up with a communication system to help operate the robot. Have three different rounds, giving everyone a chance at each role, with two minutes of planning in between each round.

TEAM BUILDING

13 14 15 16

Age Range: 13-16

Group Size: 1-5

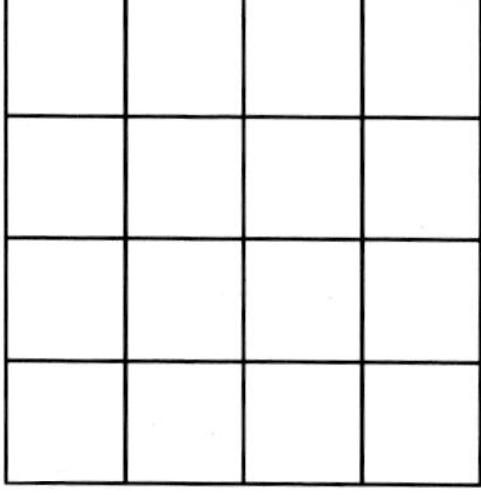

8. SQUARE CHALLENGE

This exercise is perfect for demonstrating how problem solving can be easier as a team.

Ask for a volunteer from the group and tell everyone else to be quiet. Explain to the group that the volunteer has 40 seconds to complete the puzzle.

Show the climber the 4x4 square puzzle and ask them to count the total number of squares. After 40 seconds, the climber is likely to have lost count, or got the answer wrong (the correct answer is 30).

Next, ask the climber to pick two buddies to help him solve the puzzle, and give them twenty seconds to come up with a system to count together. Start the time again, and they should be able to solve the puzzle.

Discuss how much easier this was when working together as a team, and how this is the same in competitions, or general route-reading.

TEAM BUILDING

5 6 7 8 9 10 11 12 13 14 15 16

Age Range: 5-16

Group Size: 2-20

9. TRUST FALL

This is a simple but effective team-building and bonding exercise.

Ask the climbers to get into pairs, and spread out.

Ask Climber 1 to stand behind Climber 2, and take one step back. Climber 2 must have their eyes shut the entire time.

Explain to the group that Climber 1 is going to count to three, and then Climber 2 has to fall backwards with their arms out, keeping their eyes shut. Climber 1 must catch Climber 2 as they are falling.

Explain to the group that this is a trust exercise, and Climber 1 should try to resist putting their feet down behind them.

SUSSEX
CLIMBING

CHAPTER 8

COACHING

This chapter is about developing your own techniques and skills as a climbing coach, and I hope that the following pages are thought-provoking, inspiring and useful.

There is, of course, more to being a coach then just shouting advice; in this chapter I share some of my own experiences of coaching. For more information about coaching development, please visit our website at **www.ksclimbing.co.uk/coaching**.

1. BEING A ROLE MODEL

Working with children regularly and creating a bond with them is a very satisfying job. However, a coach's responsibility doesn't finish at the end of the session. Be aware of setting a good example to your climbers – you'd be surprised how much they look up to you as a role model.

For example, imagine running your session as you normally would, starting off by reminding the group how important it is to warm up. You encourage them to begin with a pulse raiser, and to start on the easiest grades to prevent any injuries. The next day, you go climbing yourself, and one of the climbers from the session is there. They happen to be watching you, and you don't bother warming up properly because it's boring. What message does this give to that young climber? 'If my coach doesn't need to warm up, why should I?'

Always be aware of your behaviour and practices, particularly when you are around people you coach. What happens if the young climber sees you smoking or having a beer?

2. BETA IN COMPETITIONS

This is entirely my own opinion, and whilst it is definitely worth considering, it might not be the best method for everyone.

In a situation where a climber gets nervous and struggles with beta, or even panics whilst on a route, it is tempting to start shouting out beta: 'Left foot up', or 'Right heel'. A different approach would be to guide the climber towards making their own decisions, since each climber knows their own body better than anyone else.

As an example, imagine a situation when a climber gets to a tricky move. Unable to figure it out, he panics, and asks his coach for help. The coach, keen to assist, directs him with what he considers to be the best beta. Unfortunately, the beta doesn't work for this individual, who falls off and learns little from the experience.

A better approach from the coach would be to guide the climber to make their own decisions. By doing so, the climber is more likely to find a sequence that works for them, more likely to learn from the coaching, and more likely to be able to solve their own problems without coaching input in the future.

Instead of suggesting beta, ask them to take a breath and identify what the issue is. The climber may respond with something like 'I can't reach the next hold.' In that case, ask them what they could do to reach further in that direction. 'A foot-swap,' they reply. Encourage them to think deeper: 'Which type of foot-swap will work best in this situation?'

In this way, the coach encourages the climber to make their own decisions and learn from each one.

Another classic method of helping a climber to read routes is to ask them to talk you through the route before they get onto the wall.

As they describe each move, encourage them to act out their sequence, replicating the moves with their hands and feet whilst still on the floor. Encourage them to talk through every move, and even challenge them as to why they have chosen a particular move, and whether they think it is the best option.

BUILDING MUSCLE MEMORY

Building muscle memory before certain coordinated moves can be really useful. To build muscle memory, aim to repeat the motion of a move multiple times until it begin feels like habit.

For example, imagine you are about to make a powerful move to a hold that you cannot see, as it is hidden around a corner. To build muscle memory, replicate your body position, and move your hand from the starting hold to the hold you can't see, and repeat. As your spatial awareness kicks in, you should be able to eventually hit the hold with your eyes closed. Repeat this process until you are able to hit the hold every time with your eyes shut.

Make sure that your body positioning is replicating what it will be whilst you are on the wall. Having your hips six inches lower than expected may cause you to misjudge your attempt.

Another example is a step-step dyno. By standing on the mats next to the holds, and repeating the moves on the floor, you will begin to build muscle memory.

4. COMPETITION PREPARATION

When coaching a squad, competitions are obviously a big part of the job, and provide great motivation for improvement.

Goals

Before each competition season, we ask our team to set some realistic personal goals. Personally, I am a big fan of team goals too; for example, aiming for an average of 170 points per person. This inclusive method helps everyone feel like they have a role to play in the team performance.

Relieving Pressure

Too much pressure can have a negative effect, and it is useful to try to reduce pressure whenever possible. During the training session before a competition, we always let our squad have a free climbing session, often including a few fun games. We find that having a relaxed (rather than training-focused) session helps the climbers to realise that it's not as big a deal as they might think.

It can also be useful to run specific drills to help climbers prepare for competitions. These can be found in the list of *Recommended Drills* on page 189.

On the Day

Always ask the team to get to the competition early. If a competition starts at 10am, we ask everyone to be there by 8:45am. By arriving really early, the climbers have plenty of time to have a look around and get familiar with the centre.

Split the squad into groups and provide them with their own scoring sheet. Before the competition starts, have the groups walk around the centre and analyse their climbs for about 20 minutes. As they walk around the centre, ask them to give each climb a number on their scoring sheet as follows:

1 - I can definitely flash it.

2 - I think I can flash it.

3 - I think I can get it third attempt.

4 - I will leave this climb until last.

It is also useful to create a key for the location of the climbs in order to help know where each climb is. For example, *CW* stands for 'comp wall'.

A Youth Competition Squad – Competitions provide great motivation for improvement, but it's important to keep them fun.

During the Competition

During the competition, send the climbers out in groups of about three, preferably in the same groups they were in for their scoring sheet system. Each group has their own coach or volunteer – if it is a junior squad, and you have someone who is sixteen but is still part of the squad, they can be really useful as volunteer coaches.

Each coach will have the scoring sheet with them. This really helps with time management. Halfway through the competition, the coach can easily say, 'You have climb number four – a climb you know you can flash – on the comp wall, shall we try it?'

Always start with a really good warm-up, followed by an encouraging team chat. Be sure to tell the team how proud you are of them for everything they have achieved so far, and remind them of their team goals.

Keep on top of hydration and food, constantly reminding your climbers to drink water. I normally walk around approximately half way through the competition with some sugar – either chocolate bars or sweets.

5. DEALING WITH NERVES

Climbers can often get nervous before attempting a route, and it's one of our roles as coaches to be there and offer support.

Route Reading

If they are struggling to read a route, encourage them to watch other climbers first, and see what they do.

Dry Mouth

With scarier or committing climbs, begin a with a sip of water – when we are nervous or scared, our mouth goes dry, and our mind associates this with fear. By simply having a sip of water, and getting your mouth wet, you will instantly feel a lot better.

'Elvis Leg'

This is uncontrolled shaking in the legs, usually caused by a build-up of lactic acid due to prolonged muscle contraction, combined with increased activity in the nervous system due to fear.

If you notice this in one of your climbers, guide them towards dropping their heels (to reduce the muscle contraction) and taking deep, calm breaths (to relax the nervous system).

As a preventative measure, always encourage your climbers to focus on their breathing before and during each climb. Perhaps suggest that they stop briefly before a crux section and take two big breaths before continuing.

6. ENGAGING THE CORRECT FIBRES

You can read more about different types of muscle fibres and how to identify when they are required under **Strength vs Power** (page 168).

Within our muscles are two different types of muscle fibre: **fast-twitch** fibres and **slow-twitch** fibres.

Fast-twitch fibres are used for power and dynamic climbing, and slow-twitch fibres are used for strength endurance and static climbing.

Engaging the correct muscle groups before a specific type of move will increase your chance of succeeding. For example, doing a dynamic warm-up will increase your chance of feeling dynamic that session.

I use this trick in coaching all the time. A good example was during the Junior British Bouldering Championships, to which I had travelled to coach a few of our junior squad members. One squad member was attempting a dynamic problem, and although her dyno technique was spot on, she was about a foot away from the hold. She decided it was too far, but I encouraged her to have another go.

Before she did, I took her off the mats and asked her to do five star jumps, and a quick set of squat jumps, followed by some dynamic movement. She then had a sip of water to help with nerves, caught her breath, and gave it a second go. With this simple dynamic activity, we had activated her fast-twitch muscle fibres, and the effect was dramatic. Although she was unable to hang the dyno, she was now able to get her hand onto the hold – a huge improvement.

The technique also works with slow twitch fibres, which you can engage by holding gentle positions and locks – though be aware that your aim is to engage the correct muscle groups, not to get them tired.

Engaging the correct fibres – Use a tailored warm-up to engage the right kind of muscle fibres for the exercise that you're about to do.

ENGAGING MUSCLES

Engaging the right muscles is important in order to get the most out of your body for a given move. Depending on how strong your different muscle groups are, you might naturally over-engage stronger muscles, and fail to engage weaker muscles. This reduces your maximum performance and can also lead to injury.

A common example of this is people who have strong thighs but weak hamstrings and glutes. When heel hooking, these people over-engage their flagging leg and under-engage their heel hooking leg. This keeps the heel in place but makes it hard to rock over onto it, and puts a huge amount of strain on the hip flexor of the flagging leg, often causing injury.

You can feel your muscles engage with your hand. Place your hand on your bicep and tense it – it will go from soft to hard, which means the muscle is engaged. If you really tense your bicep, you will feel that muscle start to get tired. All of your climbing muscles work in the same way.

Muscle Engagement in Training

It's easy to engage the wrong muscles to complete a training exercise. Because you naturally engage the stronger muscles, you end up training those stronger muscles, and the problem of imbalance only gets worse. Not only is this training less beneficial, but you are at greater risk of injury – especially with the lower back and minor leg muscles.

Muscle Engagement on the Wall

Climbers tend to struggle to engage their leg muscles whilst actually climbing. Once they have practised engaging their muscles in floor-based exercises, encourage them to focus on engaging their legs by pulling in with their feet, and get them to practise pulling in on a heel without using the flagging leg against the wall.

To engage the lats on cut-loose moves, squeeze the elbows together. To unload the feet, engage the lats momentarily by doing a shrug. Look out for strong climbers failing on particular types of moves that they should be able to do at their level – this can often be due to muscles not being engaged correctly.

FITNESS TESTS

It is really important to keep track of a climber's progress, both for their motivation and your own understanding.

By monitoring their performance, you can see where your work has paid off, or isn't quite going to plan. This is especially useful when you are trying to plan the next training cycle.

I try to do a fitness test every twelve weeks, and it is really important to ensure it is a fair test. Be sure to provide the climbers with a thorough warm-up, and always run the test at a similar time, ideally at the beginning of a session.

I also include a benchmarking system, which highlights strengths and weaknesses and helps to determine your future training plans. You can read more about the benchmarking system online at **www.ksclimbing.co.uk/benchmark**

Example Fitness Test Score Sheet

Max pull-ups	9
Max full lock	32 seconds
Max 90 lock-off	50 seconds
Crimp dead-hang	33 seconds
One-arm hang	56 seconds
Sloper campus	1-4
Max push-ups	34
Max V-sits	45
Max L-hang	40 seconds
Max far jump	1.5 metres
Max pistol squat	3

9. FREE CLIMBING

Whether they are adults or children, climbers who are being coached to improve their climbing obviously enjoy climbing.

In groups such as squads or academies, I can imagine a lot of session plans that consist of warming-up, drills, training, and then cooling down. But I bet there are some climbers in these squads who only climb during squad sessions. If their sessions don't include any climbing, how likely are they to improve? Do they have a chance to practice the techniques that you have taught them? Also, how motivated do you think they will be if all they get to do is train?

I am obsessed with drills but I never have a session without a free climbing period in which the group can climb whatever they want. Technique, drills and training are so important to progress in climbing, but fundamentally I still believe that the best way to get better at climbing is to go climbing.

10. INJURY PREVENTION

As a coach, you have a very important role in trying to protect your climbers from injuries.

Catch Injuries Early

Always ask your climbers to inform you of anything that hurts, no matter how insignificant it seems. Don't be afraid to ask a climber to sit out for a while or miss a few sessions if you think they run the risk of getting injured. A slight ache in the elbow, or tweak in the finger, could quickly turn into something much worse, but as long as it is explained in the correct way, the climber will always prefer to miss a few hours of climbing than to be out for a few months.

Warm Up and Cool Down

Always be sure to encourage climbers to warm up properly, no matter how late they turn up. Finish every session with some stretching, and try to focus specifically on areas that you have trained. For example, if you had a triceps-intense training session, be sure to add a few extra tricep stretches at the end.

I now ensure that every session with my competition squad finishes with fifteen minutes of rehabilitation and injury prevention. These sessions make use of lacrosse balls and foam rollers for massages (to help prevent knotted muscles), and Therabands to perform TYI exercises. TYI's are amazing for increasing shoulder mobility and reducing the chance of injury. There are lots of articles about how to do TYI's online.

Advocate Rest

Understand and educate climbers about the importance of rest. If someone slightly pulls a hip flexor a week before a competition, is it wise to try and power through the niggle for the day of a competition, or does that increase the chance of it becoming a long-term injury?

Focus on Form

When training climbers, be really strict about form. If they are performing an exercise and lose form, ask them to stop.

Warm up and cool down – *A period of rehab and injury prevention at the end of a session can help to prevent the onset of injuries.*

Growth Spurts

When working regularly with young children, be hyper-aware of growth spurts.

Ask parents to measure and monitor the height of your younger climbers. In the event of a growth spurt, ensure the climbers rest and avoid any physical training. The body needs to focus its energy on growing.

If the climber is feeling exhausted for no particular reason, or they are having aches and pains within their joints and bones, it might be a sign of growing pains. A common place for growing pains to occur is in the knee joints, especially with young girls. Encourage them to climb gently and avoid jumping off as much as possible.

Large amounts of exercise can stunt growth. Try to include a few weeks of rest periods within your training plans. Avoid any form of finger training or weight training until you are sure that children have passed their growing stages.

11. KNOWING THE LINE

Recognising the line can be challenging, especially in competitions, but it is so important to consider. Remember that no competition is worth injury, and always remind the climbers that they are climbing because they enjoy climbing, not because they need to win.

An example of this is one of my proudest moments as a coach, as bizarre as it might sound. I was at a competition with my squad, and one of our squad members was battling it out for 1st place. Livvy, aged 9, had come 1st in the previous four rounds with one round to go, and was in the mindset of 'every point counts'.

I walked around the corner to see a huge audience watching and encouraging Livvy, who was halfway up a climb. She was at the top of the wall, with one move left to go, standing completely stable on a huge volume with no handholds.

Her next move was to jump to a jug, about one metre away, towards a corner. It was pretty badly set, and was incredibly dangerous for climbers of Livvy's age group.

As I approached, I noticed how everyone was encouraging her to jump, obviously recognising her ability from previous competitions. However, she looked quite distressed.

As I got close, she caught my eye and asked me to spot her.

I took a moment, and then simply responded, 'Livvy, listen. It's your decision. I will spot you and be super proud of you if you decide to go for it, but I will be even more proud of you if you tell me it's a stupid climb, and climb down.'

She climbed down, and I turned to the surprisingly disappointed crowd and demanded that they give her clap for coming down. In this instance, we both realised that it was not worth breaking a leg on this indoor climb just for a couple of points.

LESSON PLANS

This book should give you some of the tools you need to create a good session plan. Try to keep things new and fresh, and ensure that there is enough time for each part of the session. Always include a warm-up and, whenever possible, a cool-down period with time for stretching. Every session can be a great session, provided you arrive early, prep the session, demos and drills, and most importantly, have a clear objective.

Always test out your ideas or drills before using them, and be sure to think of emergency variations in case they don't suit the group. Manage group sizes by doing drill rotations. For example, have 4 groups each doing a drill for 10 minutes before rotating round. Use the session plan as a guideline, but never feel afraid to change it on the day if it isn't working. Always try to finish a session with feedback, and discuss the pros and cons of each session with your fellow coaches.

Making a Successful Lesson Plan

1) Arrive early and prep the session.

2) Start the session with a briefing.

3) Pick a warm-up and/or coordination drill.

4) Pick a technique that you would like to cover.

5) Find good demos for your chosen technique.

6) Pick some drills that relate to the chosen technique.

7) Make time for free climbing.

8) Physical training / conditioning.

9) Rehabilitation and stretching.

10) Debrief, including feedback on the session.

11) Discuss the session with other coaches.

You can read more about engaging the different types of muscle fibres on page 160.

STRENGTH vs POWER

Understanding the difference between strength and power is vital for creating a good training plan for you and your climbers, and for identifying a climber's strengths and weaknesses.

Strength and Power

Strength, on the other hand, is concerned purely with the amount of force that you can apply with your muscles at a given instant. It is worth noting that strength itself is very complex, and that there are different types of strength. However, most climbers tend to use the term strength to describe maximum strength or strength endurance.

Power is the ability to generate force as fast as possible (*Power = Force x Speed*). Power is important to us in dynamic climbing.

Notice that strength begins with an **S**, which is going to help us remember how to link everything that follows. Strength is important and is used to climb **statically**.

Muscle Contractions

There are two different types of muscle contraction: **isometric** contractions (in which the muscle is engaged but not moving, such as when holding a plank position), and **isotonic** contractions (in which the muscle is engaged and moving, such as during a pull-up). We don't have the **S** to look for here, but an easy way to remember which one is which is to think of isometric as being like **isame**tric, with the muscles staying the **same** and not moving.

Application to Climbing

Imagine a climber is doing a rockover, and is fully locked off. This is a slow, static move during an isometric contraction, meaning it is a strength-based move.

Now imagine a climber is performing a dyno. This is a quick, dynamic move during an isotonic muscle contraction, meaning it is a power-based move.

Understanding this difference helps us to identify which training exercises develop which attribute. Generally, if the exercise is slow, it is strength-based. If it is quick, it is power-based. For example, holding a locked position for five seconds on a pull-up bar will require and build strength, whereas doing a clap pull-up will require and build power. Similarly, doing a push-up at slow to normal speed will require strength, but doing a clap push-up will call upon power.

Strength and Power – *As a climber, it is useful to have and train both of these different attributes. A basic understanding of these concepts can help to identify relevant exercises for specific climbing moves.*

14. WIN-WIN / WIN-LOSE ATTITUDES

A positive mental attitude can go a long way in training, particularly in relation to goal-setting. More importantly, in most situations you can chose to adopt a **win-win** attitude, or a **win-lose** attitude.

For example, imagine you came 10th in round 1 of a competition, and you set a goal to come 3rd by round 3. In between the rounds, you trained really hard, with admirable focus, and in round 2 you came 4th.

Now you could, at this point, take a **win-lose** attitude. If you come 3rd, you win because you hit your goal; if you come 4th, you lose, because you didn't come 3rd and missed your goal.

The other option is to take the **win-win** attitude. If you come 3rd, you win because you hit your goal. If you come 4th, you still actually win, because you were 10th a month ago. If you hadn't set yourself a goal, it's likely you wouldn't have trained so hard, and you would probably still be 10th!

15. WORDING

Choosing the right words can make an unbelievable difference. As a coach, you have the opportunity to say the right thing and make a bad situation great, or to say the wrong thing and make a good situation bad.

Positive Framing

Always try to focus on talking positively. Your positivity creates belief and motivation. Eliminate the failure and turn everything into a positive. For example, if a climber in a competition attempts a dyno, latches the hold but falls off and looks at you, respond with something like, 'Awesome, you know you can get the height! Now we just need to hold the swing.'

Try to avoid negative words like '*but*' or '*however*' when giving feedback. For example, if you say, 'Great session; your flagging is perfect, but we still need to improve your smearing', the climber is more likely to walk away disappointed about their smearing than happy about their flagging.

A better thing to say is, 'Great session, your flagging is perfect, and your smearing has improved ten-fold. Shall we make it perfect next week?'

This simple change of wording will leave the climber buzzed about their flagging and smearing, and keen to put in that extra work to improve.

Positivity and Reassurance

Constantly prompt yourself and your climbers to be positive, and remind them of how well they are doing. Highlight their achievements and reassure them that being nervous is very normal.

One of my squad was at the BMC Youth Series Final, and told me that she was really nervous. I responded by saying, 'Yeah! You made it to the finals, it's OK to be nervous! I'm nervous for you. But you could come last today and I'd still be incredibly proud of you for making it to the finals in your first year – what an achievement!'

It takes a bit of practice, but always focus on your wording; it really makes a big difference.

Explain Rather than Tell...

Always try to explain *why* you are asking your climbers to do something, rather than just telling them to do it. If possible, explain why it is going to be beneficial for their climbing. For example: 'Can we do five squat jumps, please? Squat jumps are really useful for climbing, as they help us generate power from our legs.'

Allow People to Impress

Although I always avoid lying to my clients, I must admit that it can be beneficial to bend the truth a little in order to boost their confidence. An example of this is asking a climber to do five pull-ups, and saying that you will be really impressed if they can, when in reality you already know that they are capable of doing ten. This leaves room for some positive feedback.

Another example of this is with a climber I coach, who struggles to rest properly in between climbs. Sometimes, if I feel that he hasn't rested enough, I will walk over to him when he is about to get onto a climb, and start telling him jokes, or asking him to try and slap my hand whilst I move it away. He views this as me just being silly, but I'm actually helping him to achieve the rest that he needs to perform well.

CHAPTER 9

RESOURCES

In this chapter, I have included checklists of all of the drills and techniques included in this book. These can be photocopied and used to keep track of which exercises you have completed with a particular coaching group.

I have also included **Strength & Weakness Charts**, which are a useful tool for analysing and developing a climber's technique. To use the charts, ask a climber to shade in each section according to how confident they feel in that area. For example, if they are 100% happy with their ability to foot-swap, they shade in the whole of that section. If they are only 20% confident in this area, then they shade roughly 20% of the area, and so on.

Doing this can provide both coach and climber with areas to work on and goals to aim for. After about 6 weeks, ask the climbers to fill in the charts again and see where more work is still needed.

WARM-UP CHECKLIST

Group :

Tick off or date the group warm-up exercises once completed with a particular coaching group.

WARM-UPS

☐	1. Arm Bridge Challenge	10
☐	2. Back to Back	10
☐	3. Boot Wars	10
☐	4. Bunny Hops Race	11
☐	5. Finger Wars	11
☐	6. Foot Wars	12
☐	7. Frog Jumps	12
☐	8. Fun Pulse Raiser	13
☐	9. Help Ups	13
☐	10. The Human Chair	14
☐	11. Human Drag Race	14
☐	12. Human Plank Challenge	15
☐	13. Human Pyramid	15
☐	14. Killer	15
☐	15. Mirror Dance	16
☐	16. Monkeying Around	16
☐	17. Obstacle Course	16
☐	18. Skipping Ropes	17
☐	19. Standard Warm-up	17
☐	20. Step Wars	18
☐	21. Wheelbarrow Race	18

COORDINATION DRILLS CHECKLIST

Group :

Tick off or date the coordination drills once completed with a particular coaching group.

COORDINATION DRILLS

TECHNIQUES CHECKLIST

Group :

Tick off or date the techniques once completed with a particular coaching group.

CLIMBING TECHNIQUES

Level	Checkbox	Technique	Page
Beginner		1. Legs are Stronger than Arms!	36
		2. Shifting Weight	36
		3. Straight Arms	37
		4. Twisting	37
Novice		5. Basic Flagging	38
		6. Bridging	40
		7. Foot Placements	41
		8. Foot Swaps	42
		9. Smearing	43
Intermediate		10. Drop Knees	44
		11. Dynos	46
		12. Flagging – Back Flags	48
		13. Flagging – Inside Flags	48
		14. Heel Hooks	50
		15. Mantles	52
		16. Palming	52
		17. Rockovers	53
		18. Toe Hooks	54
Advanced		19. Breathing	56
		20. Campusing	56
		21. The Campus Swing	58
		22. Cutting Loose	58
		23. Dynamic Foot Smear	60
		24. Pulling in with Feet	60
		25. Route Reading	61
		26. Scary Moves – Bat Hangs	62
		27. Scary Moves – Knee Bars	64
		28. Scary Moves – Running Starts	64
		29. Scary Moves – Step-Step Dynos	65
		30. Scary Moves – Step-Step Kicks	66
		31. Windmills	66

DRILLS CHECKLIST

Group :

Tick off or date the drills once completed with a particular coaching group.

IMPROVER DRILLS

Level	Done	Drill	Page
Beginner		1. Good & Bad Placements	70
		2. Beanbag on Heads	70
		3. Foot Swap Every Move	70
		4. Hover Feet	71
		5. Hover Hands	71
		6. Mat Trust	71
		7. Ninja Feet	72
		8. Ninja Feet 2	72
		9. No Foot Swapping	73
		10. No Matching	73
		11. Octopus Feet	73
		12. Octopus Hands	74
		13. Point and Go	74
		14. Stickers Shifting	74
		15. Stop! 1,2,3	75
Novice		16. Beanbag Challenge	75
		17. Boxing Gloves	76
		18. Bumping	77
		19. Cork & Beanbag Elimination	77
		20. Corks on Footholds	77
		21. Double Footed	78
		22. Double Handed	78
		23. Double Hand & Foot	78
		24. Elimination	79
		25. Foot to Hand	79
		26. Footwork Tape	80
		27. Footwork Test	80
		28. Flagging Line	81
		29. Flag Happy	81
		30. Heel to Hand	82
		31. Match Every Hold	83
		32. No Foot Adjustments	84

DRILLS CHECKLIST

Group :

Tick off or date the drills once completed with a particular coaching group.

IMPROVER DRILLS

DRILLS CHECKLIST

Group :

Tick off or date the drills once completed with a particular coaching group.

IMPROVER DRILLS

DRILLS CHECKLIST

Group :

Tick off or date the drills once completed with a particular coaching group.

IMPROVER DRILLS

Advanced

	Drill	Page
☐	97. Foot Taps (Dynamic)	114
☐	98. Golf	114
☐	99. Hand Taps (Dynamic)	115
☐	100. Hand Taps (Static)	115
☐	101. Hover 90°	116
☐	102. Hover Lock and Move	117
☐	103. No Feet	117
☐	104. Peer Objectives	118
☐	105. Perfect Climb	118
☐	106. Points Constant Ladder	118
☐	107. Points Ladder	119
☐	108. Points Race	120
☐	109. Race Game	120
☐	110. Recognition	120
☐	111. Red Flag Style	121
☐	112. Roof Cut Loose	122
☐	113. Roof Heel-Toe Match	123
☐	114. Roof Hooking	123
☐	115. Roof Pinning	124
☐	116. Route-Reading Analysis	124
☐	117. Route-Reading Discussion	125
☐	118. Setting Problems	125
☐	119. Straight Arm Campus	126
☐	120. Swing Challenge	126
☐	121. Swing Square	126
☐	122. Teaching	127
☐	123. Team Pressure	128
☐	124. Technique Analysis	128
☐	125. Tech Flags Only	129
☐	126. Tired Core	129
☐	127. Windmill Drill	129
☐	128. Yo-yos	130

GROUP MANAGEMENT

GROUP MANAGEMENT CHECKLIST

Group :

Tick off or date the group-management exercises once completed with a particular coaching group.

☐	1. Beanbag Fetch	134
☐	2. Blindfold Ninja	134
☐	3. Blindfold Tags	134
☐	4. Buddy Checks	135
☐	5. Climbing!	135
☐	6. Getting Dressed	136
☐	7. Long Traversing Game	136
☐	8. Itchy Head	137
☐	9. Safety Triangle	137

GAMES

GAMES CHECKLIST

Group :

Tick off or date the games once completed with a particular coaching group.

☐	1. Blindfold Tag Game	140
☐	2. Climbing Dodge Ball	140
☐	3. Coach Says	140
☐	4. Climbing Twister	141
☐	5. Dead-Hang Challenge	141
☐	6. Hang Tough	141
☐	7. Mountain Valley Cave	142
☐	8. Musical Climbers	142
☐	9. Noodle Obstacles	142
☐	10. Relay Race	143
☐	11. Rock Warriors	143
☐	12. Shark Attack	144
☐	13. Sock Wrestling	144

TEAM-BUILDING CHECKLIST

TEAM-BUILDING

Group :

Tick off or date the games once completed with a particular coaching group.

STRENGTHS & WEAKNESSES
BEGINNER & NOVICE

Name :

Shade in each segment to show roughly how confident / skilled you feel in that technique.

For example, if you are 100% confident in a particular technique, shade in the whole segment.

Use the chart to identify areas to work on, and to set training goals.

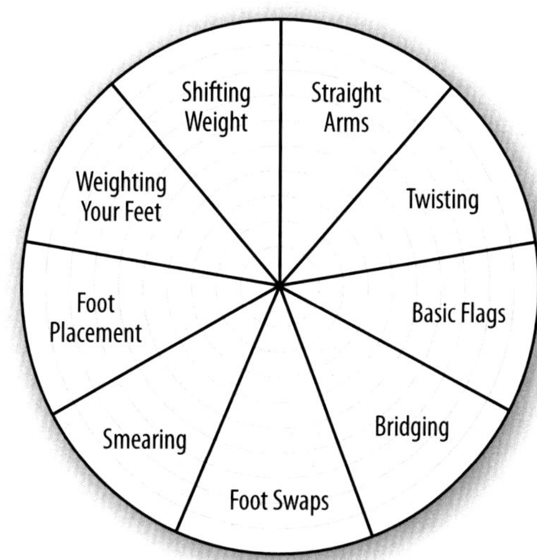

STRENGTHS & WEAKNESSES
INTERMEDIATE

Name :

Shade in each segment to show roughly how confident / skilled you feel in that technique.

For example, if you are 100% confident in a particular technique, shade in the whole segment.

Use the chart to identify areas to work on, and to set training goals.

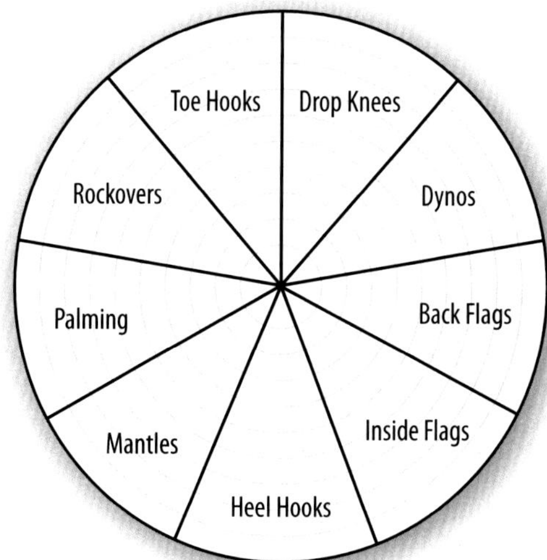

STRENGTHS & WEAKNESSES

ADVANCED

Name :

Shade in each segment to show roughly how confident / skilled you feel in that technique.

For example, if you are 100% confident in a particular technique, shade in the whole segment.

Use the chart to identify areas to work on, and to set training goals.

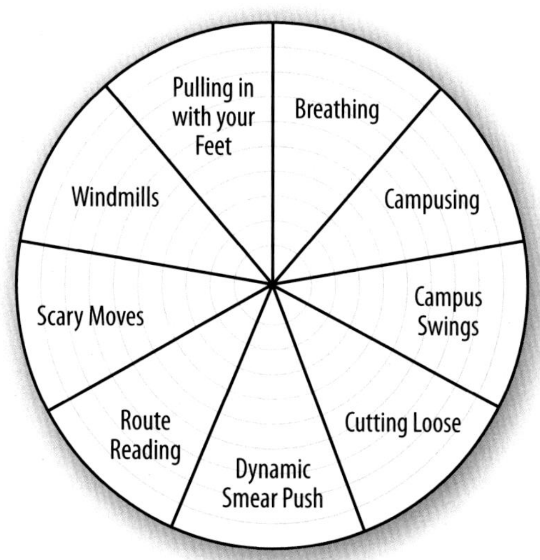

STRENGTHS & WEAKNESSES
PHYSICAL 1

Name :

Shade in each segment to show roughly how confident / skilled you feel in that technique.

For example, if you are 100% confident in a particular technique, shade in the whole segment.

Use the chart to identify areas to work on, and to set training goals.

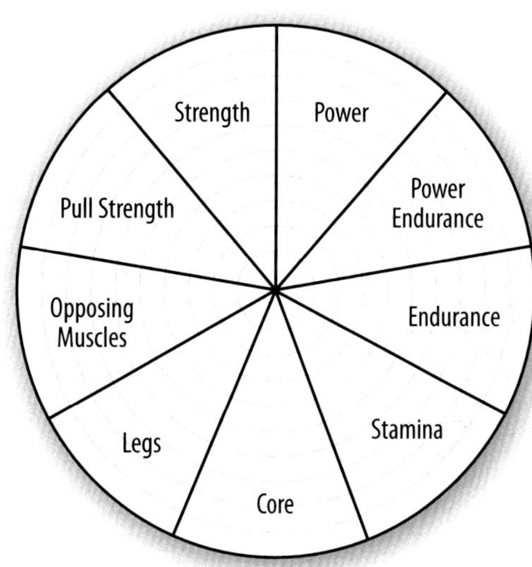

STRENGTHS & WEAKNESSES
PHYSICAL 2

Name :

Shade in each segment to show roughly how confident / skilled you feel in that technique.

For example, if you are 100% confident in a particular technique, shade in the whole segment.

Use the chart to identify areas to work on, and to set training goals.

MALE
7
FEMALE
7
JUNIOR GIRLS
7
SUSSEX
CLIMBING
TEAM

CHAPTER 10

RECOMMENDED DRILLS

In this chapter we provide some recommended drills for general aspects of climbing, including dynamic drills to activate fast-twitch muscle fibres, static drills to work slow-twitch muscles, and recommended drills for developing strength, power, and endurance.

We have also included a list of recommended drills for each of the climbing techniques described in Chapter 3.

RECOMMENDED DRILLS
DYNAMIC

RECOMMENDED DRILLS
STATIC

RECOMMENDED DRILLS
STRENGTH

RECOMMENDED DRILLS
POWER

RECOMMENDED DRILLS
POWER ENDURANCE & ENDURANCE

4x4 Climbing	89	Points Ladder	119
Add a Move	89	Points Race	120
Cut – 1, 2, 3	112	Red Flag Style	121
Mileage	97	Set Ladder	102
Perfect Climb	118	Yoyos	130
Points Constant Ladder	118		

RECOMMENDED DRILLS
COMPETITION PREPARATION

Adjusting Holds	90	Down Climb	93
Anxiety Prep	106	Recognition	120
Bad Beta	108	Team Pressure	128
Blindfolded Route Reading	91	Wrong Positions	105
Competition	111		

RECOMMENDED DRILLS
CONFIDENCE BUILDING

Mat Trust	71	Recognition	120
Mileage	97	Teaching	127

RECOMMENDED DRILLS
OVERHANG

4x4 Climbing	89	No Feet	117
Avoid the Cut	108	Pulling with Feet	101
Cut – 1, 2, 3	112	Roof Battle	102
Feet Pulling	95	Roof Hooking	123
Foot Swap on Board	113	Roof Hug	102
Foot Taps (Dynamic)	114	Straight Arm Campus	126
Foot Taps	113		

RECOMMENDED DRILLS
ROOF

Avoid the Cut	108	Roof Cut Loose	122
Bat Hang Climbing	110	Roof Heel-Toe Match	123
Cut – 1, 2, 3	112	Roof Hooking	123
Dizzy Climbing	112	Roof Pinning	124
Feet Pulling	95	Straight Arm Campus	126
No Feet	117	Swing Challenge	126
Pulling with Feet	101	Swing Square	126

RECOMMENDED DRILLS
SLAB

Balance Traverse	90	Heel to Hand	82
Beanbag on Heads	70	Palm Every Move	99
Boxing Gloves	76	Point and Go	74
Down Climb	93	Pulling with Feet	101
Feet Pulling	95	Restricted Arms	101
Foot to Hand	79	Yoyos	130

RECOMMENDED DRILLS
VERTICAL / FACE

Adjusting Holds	90	Pivoting a Foot	99
Clockwork	93	Pulling with Feet	101
Down Climb	93	Smear a Foot	86
Feet Pulling	95	Smear, Smear, Step	86
Foot to Hand	79	Technical Flags Only	129
Heel to Hand	82	Traverse Challenge	88

RECOMMENDED DRILLS
BEGINNER TECHNIQUES

Legs are Stronger than Arms

Good & Bad Placements	70	Point and Go	74
Balance Traverse	90	Restricted Arms	101
Boxing Gloves	76	Rounded Hands	86
Feet Pulling	95	Stickers Shifting	74
No Hands!	84	Weighted Feet Means Rest!	88

Shifting Weight

Balance Traverse	90	No Hands!	84
Boxing Gloves	76	Point and Go	74
Feet Pulling	95	Restricted Arms	101
Heel Hook Rockovers	96	Rounded Hands	86
Hover Feet	71	Slab Octopus	103
Hover Hands	71	Stickers Shifting	74

Straight Arms

Feet Pulling	95	Pulling with Feet	101
Hover Feet	71	Starting Positions	104
Hover Hands	71	Traverse Challenges	88
Match Every Hold	83		

Twisting

Flagging Line	81	Octopus Feet	73
Flag Happy	81	Octopus Hands	74
Hand Taps (Dynamic)	115	Traverse Challenges	88
Hand Taps (Static)	115		

Basic Flagging

Flagging Line	81	No Foot Swapping	73
Flag Happy	81	No Matching	73
Hover Hands	71	Technique Analysis	128

RECOMMENDED DRILLS
NOVICE TECHNIQUES

Bridging

Hover Feet	71	Weighted Feet Means Rest!	88
No Hands!	84	Wrong Positions	105
Points Constant Ladder	118		

Footwork

Good & Bad Placements	70	Ninja Feet	72
Cork & Beanbag Elimination	77	Ninja Feet 2	72
Corks on footholds	77	No Foot Adjustments	84
Down Climb	93	Pivoting a Foot	99
Feet Pulling	95	Pulling with Feet	101
Foot to Hand	79	Roof Pinning	124
Footwork Competition	95	Stab and Go	104
Footwork Tape	80	Sticky Eyes	87
Footwork Test	80	Technique Analysis	128
Hover Feet	71	Tired Core	129

RECOMMENDED DRILLS
INTERMEDIATE TECHNIQUES

RECOMMENDED DRILLS
ADVANCED TECHNIQUES

Toe Hooks

Breathing

Campusing

Campus Swing

Cutting Loose

Dynamic Smear Push

Pulling in with Feet

Route Reading

Scary Moves

Windmills

NOTES

NOTES

Oxford Alpine Club Guidebooks
www.oxfordalpineclub.co.uk

Rjukan | Selected Ice Climbs

A modern photo topo guide to 200 of the best roadside ice climbs in Norway's famous Rjukan valley, including all of the popular climbing areas and full background information.

Published 2017

ISBN: 978-0-9935486-4-2

Todra | Rock Climbing in the Todra Gorge

Lying on the southern fringe of the High Atlas is one of Morocco's premier climbing destinations – the magnificent Todra Gorge. Here, bathed in year-round sunshine, you will find a climbing experience like few others: an enticing blend of sport, adventure, and exotic culture...

3rd edition published 2019

ISBN: 978-0-9935486-8-0

Climb Tafraout | Moroccan Anti-Atlas

Morocco's Anti-Atlas mountains are a paradise of adventurous traditional climbing, where winter sun, stunning scenery and an enchanting culture combine to create one of the world's most exciting climbing destinations. This new guide includes 1500 of the very best routes across the range.

Published 2017

ISBN: 978-0-9935486-2-8

Climb Tafraout | Tafraout Granite

The definitive guide to Tafraout's granite cragging, detailing almost 250 routes from single-pitch sport climbs to multi-pitch trad routes on the incredible granite domes around Tafraout and Aguerd Oudad.

Published 2018

ISBN: 978-0-9935486-5-9

Setesdal | Ice Climbing in Norway's Setesdal and Åseral Regions

Home to more than 150 superb icefalls, ranging from roadside top-ropes to full-on multi-pitch adventures, the Setesdal region of southern Norway offers a serious alternative to the busier Rjukan Valley. This pocket guide describes all the main routes and full background information.

Published 2012

ISBN: 978-0-9567288-1-4

Climb Tafraout | 100 Classic Climbs

With a focus on multi-pitch routes and mountain adventures, this lavish guidebook describes 100 of the very best climbs in Morocco's Anti-Atlas mountains. Super-detailed photo topos, maps and full route descriptions provide all the information you need to enjoy some of the best mountain rock in Morocco.

1st edition published 2018

ISBN: 978-0-9935486-6-6